Series editor: Alan White

THE WEIMAR REPUBLIC

Alan White

Collins Educational

Published by CollinsEducational
An imprint of HarperCollins*Publishers*
77-85 Fulham Palace Road
London W6 8JB

© HarperCollins*Publishers* 1997

First published 1997
Reprinted 1997, 1998

ISBN 0 00 327276-1

Alan White asserts the moral right to be identified as the author of this work.

British Library Cataloguing in Publication Data
A catalogue record for this book is available from the British Library.

Acknowledgements

The author wishes to express his gratitude to his colleague, Adrian Berger, for commenting on successive drafts of this book.

The author and publishers are grateful to the following for permission to reproduce illustrative material.

British Library (pp. 27, 30)

Cover photograph: A 300 mark stamp from 1923, overstamped as a 2 million mark stamp. Courtesy of Stanley Gibbons Ltd.

Edited by Lorimer Poultney
Design by Derek Lee
Illustrations by John Booth
Production by Susan Cashin

Printed and bound by
Scotprint Limited, Musselburgh

Contents

1 *Introduction*

Government and society in Germany before 1918

The Imperial Constitution

The German Empire which collapsed in 1918 was less than 50 years old. Created in 1871, it consisted of the kingdom of Prussia, ruled by the Hohenzollern dynasty, and 24 lesser states: three smaller kingdoms (Bavaria, Saxony and Württemberg), 18 principalities and three free cities. These lesser states had not joined the Empire voluntarily but had been forced into membership of it by Prussia. The term 'unification' is often used to describe the developments which led to the Empire's creation but 'Prussification' is a better description of what happened. Prussia dominated the German Empire in every way. It accounted for two-thirds of the Empire's land area and two-thirds of its population. Under the imperial constitution of 1871 Prussia's king was also Germany's Kaiser (emperor).

To outward appearance the German Empire was not a straightforwardly autocratic state like its neighbour to the east, Tsarist Russia. Germany had its Kaiser but it also had a high-profile imperial parliament (*Reichstag*) elected on the basis of universal suffrage. The Reichstag's powers, however, were limited. It could not initiate legislation: it could only reject or amend proposals handed down to it by the *Bundesrat* (Federal Council), a body composed of representatives of the Empire's member states and effectively controlled by the Kaiser. More important, government ministers, chief of whom was the Imperial Chancellor, were not in any way accountable to the Reichstag. Government ministers were appointed by the Kaiser and kept office as long as they retained his confidence.

The Reichstag's powerlessness led Wilhelm Liebknecht, in the 1870s one of the founders of Germany's Social Democratic Party, to describe it as 'a fig leaf covering the nakedness of absolutism'. Eduard David, another pre-war socialist leader, called the Reichstag a 'sham parliament'. In practice political power in Germany rested with the Kaiser and his government. 'There is only one master in this country', proclaimed Wilhelm II, Germany's emperor 1888–1918, 'That am I'.

Political tensions

The Kaiser's regime was backed by a number of powerful élites in German society. Notable among them were the Prussian landed class (the *Junkers*), the senior officers of the German army, the majority of whom were of aristocratic or *Junker* origin, the bureaucrats of the Prussian civil service and the industrial tycoons and financiers who rose to prominence on the back of the explosive economic growth which took place after 1880. Together these élites formed the ruling class of Imperial Germany.

In the years before 1914 Germany's ruling class came to see the Social Democratic Party (the *Sozialdemokratische Partei Deutschlands* – SPD) as the principal threat to its position. Nominally the SPD was a Marxist party. Its Erfurt Programme (1891) committed it to the establishment of socialism by revolutionary means. In practice, though, the SPD was for the most part reformist rather than revolutionary. It sought to advance the socialist cause by lawful methods and focused its efforts on building a power base within the Reichstag. After 1890, drawing on the support of Germany's fast-growing urban working class, the SPD made rapid headway and in 1912 became – much to the alarm of the ruling class – the largest single party in the Reichstag.

Religious divisions

German society was divided by religion as well as by social class. The pre-war German Empire was largely Protestant, but contained a 20-million strong Catholic minority. Northern and central Germany were largely Protestant and parts of west and south Germany strongly Catholic. Catholics were viewed with suspicion by Prussia's Protestant ruling class. In the 1870s they had angered Bismarck (Imperial Chancellor, 1871–90) by forming their own political party, the *Zentrum* (Centre Party). Bismarck, fearing that the *Zentrum* would become a standard-bearer for all opponents of Prussian dominance within the new Empire, responded by launching the so-called *Kulturkampf* or 'cultural struggle', a campaign designed to intimidate and weaken the Catholic Church in Germany. The *Kulturkampf* was abandoned in the 1880s but it left a legacy of bitterness behind it. In 1914 positions of real influence in the state were still largely closed to Catholics.

The war which broke out in 1914 was fought by the German ruling class in order to further its own interests. It aimed not only to destroy its enemies abroad (especially Russia) before they became too powerful but also to undermine the growing appeal of socialism at home. Despite the fact that the war was not of their making, Germany's other social classes rallied to its support. A wave of patriotic enthusiasm swept across the country. Political differences were set aside. A political truce, known as the *Burgfriede*, was agreed. 'I know no parties any more, only Germans', declared Wilhelm II in August 1914.

The German Revolution 1918–19

How was the Weimar Republic established, and how serious was the threat to its existence from the left?

Key points

◆ In October 1918 parliamentary government replaced autocracy in Germany

◆ The political system established in October lasted only a few weeks before a popular revolution took place. In November 1918 Germany's socialists monopolised political power but were divided on the issue of what kind of political system to create

◆ The Spartacist revolt aimed to make Germany a soviet, rather than a democratic, republic

◆ The Majority Socialists were forced to enlist the support of right-wing paramilitaries in order to suppress the extreme left

◆ The 1919 constitution was democratic but flawed

What was the 'revolution from above' in October 1918?

In 1914 and after Germans were assured by the army's High Command that victory was certain. By 1917 these assurances had worn thin. The Allied naval blockade had begun to bite hard. Food supplies had run short. Political discontent began to surface. In July 1917 the SPD and the Centre Party put forward a resolution in the Reichstag calling for a compromise peace with the Allies. This 'peace resolution' was passed by 212–126 votes.

The army's last gamble for victory

The Bolshevik seizure of power in Petrograd in November 1917 offered the High Command one last hope of outright victory. The Bolsheviks, inheritors of a country with a war-weary populace and a mutinous army, were desperate to end Russia's war with Germany. Peace talks opened in late 1917 and led to the Treaty of Brest-Litovsk (March 1918). Under Brest-Litovsk Germany gained huge tracts of territory in eastern Europe but these gains were not as important at the time as the treaty's strategic benefits. Brest-Litovsk allowed Germany to scale down its military operations in eastern Europe and to concentrate its efforts on the Western Front.

In March–July 1918 Germany's armies in France launched a series of major offensives together codenamed 'Operation Michael'. The Allied armies buckled but did not break. In August they counter-attacked and began steadily to gain ground. In September Germany's army chiefs – Paul von Hindenburg, head of the High Command, and Erich Ludendorff, his senior quartermaster-general – recognised that the war had been lost.

The actions of the army leaders

The prime concern of Hindenburg and Ludendorff at this point was to protect the reputation of the German army. They set out to ensure that responsibility for defeat would be shouldered not by the High Command but by civilian politicians. In late September 1918 Ludendorff told the Kaiser that Germany should sue for peace. He further advised that a new government should be formed consisting of the leaders of the main parties in the Reichstag. Wilhelm II, who had effectively surrendered control over political and military affairs to the High Command back in 1916, accepted Ludendorff's advice. On 1 October Prince Max of Baden, head of the German Red Cross and a political moderate, was appointed Imperial Chancellor. The members of Prince Max's new government included Matthias Erzberger of the Centre Party and Philipp Scheidemann and Gustav Bauer of the SPD.

The political changes of October 1918 were of immense significance. Germany ceased to be an autocracy and became a parliamentary democracy on the British model. The Kaiser had been turned into a constitutional monarch, shorn of any real power. Significantly, though, the change had been brought about solely by the interests of the High Command and not through pressures exerted by the German people. It is for this reason that the events of October 1918 have been described by historians as a 'revolution from above'.

The behaviour of Hindenburg and Ludendorff in the autumn of 1918 was shameful. The Reichstag politicians, by contrast, behaved extraordinarily well. They knew when they took office that the military situation was hopeless. They were aware, as one SPD leader put it, that they were taking over a 'bankrupt enterprise', but they did not shrink from doing what they believed to be their patriotic duty.

Those responsible for the 'revolution from above' may have hoped that it would allow the Kaiser to continue to reign, though not to rule. If so, they were mistaken. Woodrow Wilson, the United States President, made it clear in October 1918 that the Allies were unwilling to negotiate with Germany while the Kaiser remained in place. Wilhelm II thus came to be seen within Germany as a major obstacle to peace. The pressure on him to go began to mount.

The November revolution

On 28 October 1918, Admiral Reinhard Scheer, chief of the Naval High Command, acting without authority from Prince Max's government, ordered Germany's High Seas Fleet to put to sea. His aim was to strike one last blow at the British. Scheer's order proved to be the catalyst of revolution.

The High Seas Fleet left port amid rumours that it was being sent on a suicide attack. The attitude of the Fleet's sailors to this possibility soon became clear. On 30 October the crews of two cruisers, the *Thüringen* and the *Helgoland*, refused to obey orders. The Fleet was forced to return to its base at

Kiel. Once it was back in harbour the mutiny spread. On 2 November a mass meeting of 20,000 sailors and workers at Kiel called for the establishment of a German republic and passed a resolution setting up a workers' and sailors' council or soviet.

From Kiel the revolution spread rapidly across Germany. Workers' and soldiers' councils were set up in Hamburg (6 November), Cologne (7 November), Frankfurt, Leipzig and Munich (8 November) and finally Berlin (9 November). Imperial authority collapsed abruptly and completely. By 9 November the whole of Germany was effectively in the hands of socialist-controlled soviets.

The pressure on the Kaiser now became overwhelming. On 9 November he fled to Holland (where he died, aged 82, in 1941). It was the first major development on what was to prove an exceptionally crowded day. The second casualty on 9 November was Prince Max's five-week-old multi-party government. Warned by Germany's moderate socialist leaders that they could lose control of the revolutionary movement to extremists unless an exclusively socialist administration came into being, Prince Max handed over power to a six-man socialist government headed by the SPD leader Friedrich Ebert, a modest and decent but unexciting former journalist and party organiser. The third major event of 9 November was the proclamation of a German republic from the balcony of the Reichstag building by the socialist Philipp Scheidemann. Two days later, on 11 November, an armistice was agreed with the Allies.

Divisions among the socialists

At this point the mastery of Germany's socialists over their country was more or less complete. Its future was theirs to decide. They were, however, divided among themselves.

In April 1917, more than 18 months before the November revolution, a major rift had opened in the SPD's ranks. A minority, headed by Hugo Haase, broke away from the SPD proper to form the Independent Social Democrats (the *Unabhängige Sozialdemokratische Partei Deutschlands* – USPD). Essentially the breakaway was the result of attitudes to the war: the USPD came out openly against the war while the SPD proper, sometimes called the Majority Socialists, continued to support it. The split was certainly not a straightforward left-right one: some USPD members, such as Eduard Bernstein, before 1914 the foremost theorist of a 'reformist' socialism in Germany, were on political issues other than the war as moderate as any of the Majority Socialist leaders. By and large, though, the USPD did attract the more left-wing and militant elements of the socialist movement. Associated with the USPD, for example, were the radical grassroots leaders (shop stewards) of the factory workers of Berlin and other major cities, headed by Emil Barth. Also associated with the USPD in 1917–18 was a small faction led by Karl Liebknecht and the formidable Polish-born socialist theorist Rosa Luxemburg calling itself the Spartacus League. In December 1918 the Spartacus League split away from the USPD and renamed itself the German Communist Party (*Kommunistische Partei Deutschlands* – KPD).

The government formed by Ebert on 9 November 1918 contained members of both the USPD and the Majority Socialists. They were, though, far from united about the way forward. There were, broadly speaking, two political strategies open to German socialists in late 1918. One, favoured by the Majority Socialists, was to establish a parliamentary democracy and the other, supported by left-wingers in the USPD and by the Spartacus League, was to create a soviet republic. When the Majority Socialists called for a democratically-elected Constituent Assembly, the function of which would be to draw up a new constitution, left-wingers objected, arguing that within such an Assembly anti-socialist representatives of the middle and upper classes would have a powerful voice in the making of the new Germany. Left-wingers wanted to ensure that post-imperial Germany would be a socialist Germany, and for this reason argued that the new political system should be based on the workers' and soldiers' councils which had sprung up in November 1918. The objection to a soviet-based system, in the eyes of the Majority Socialists, was that legitimacy would be lacking: political arrangements would be imposed on the German people without their consent.

Germany's socialists argued out their differences at the National Congress of German Workers' and Soldiers' Councils in Berlin in mid-December 1918. Delegates from all the soviets that had been formed a month earlier, most of them Majority Socialists, were present. On 19 December the Majority Socialists routed the left when the Congress voted 344–98 to hold elections for a Constituent Assembly. The elections were scheduled for 19 January 1919.

The Spartacist revolt and the Freikorps

The outcome of the December Congress was viewed with dismay by militant socialists and in particular by members of the Spartacus League. The Spartacists feared that a once and for all opportunity to create a socialist Germany was being allowed to slip away. Rather than allow this to happen they were prepared to seize power by force. On 6 January 1919 Spartacist units occupied newspaper offices, government buildings and railway stations in Berlin.

The impetus behind the attempted seizure of power by the Spartacus League (or German Communist Party as it was after 31 December 1918) came from its rank and file rather than its leaders. Liebknecht and Luxemburg recognised that the Spartacists were too few in number to seize power – one estimate by a foreign visitor suggested that there were no more than 5,000 Spartacists in Berlin in early 1919 – but once the revolt began in earnest they worked tirelessly for its success.

A Communist uprising was an event which Germany's middle and upper classes and Ebert's government had both feared and anticipated. Not surprisingly, contingency plans had been laid. These originated with the so-called 'Ebert–Groener pact' of 10 November 1918. The pact was the result of an approach made to Ebert by General Wilhelm Groener, Ludendorff's successor as quartermaster-general of the German army. Groener offered Ebert the army's support in upholding order if the Chancellor in return promised to use his authority to maintain discipline in the armed forces. Ebert accepted.

Following the 10 November pact, Groener moved nine regular army divisions into Berlin to maintain public order. It soon became clear, however, that these units were unreliable. This was the result of the 'Marstall episode'. The Marstall were the stables of the former royal palace. In mid-November 1918 they were occupied by a detachment of radical sailors calling themselves the People's Naval Division. In December an attempt by Groener's troops to turn the Naval Division out of the Marstall failed because his nine divisions had been reduced by desertions to a mere 800 men. With the regular army unreliable, Groener concluded that irregular forces would have to be raised if order

VOLUNTEERS	COMRADES
FLAME THROWER PERSONNEL	The Spartacus danger has not yet been removed Can you look on this with calm?
Enlist in the Flame Thrower Section of	
THE LUTTEWITZ CORPS	**NO!**
	Think of what your dead comrades would think
	Soldiers, arise
Immediate pay plus 5 marks daily bonus	Prevent Germany from becoming the laughing stock of the earth *Enrol now in*
FREE FOOD AND EQUIPMENT	The Huelsen Free Corps

Figure 1
Translations of Free Corps recruiting posters

were to be maintained. His views were shared by Gustav Noske, a tough right-wing Majority Socialist who had joined Ebert's government as defence minister in late December after its three USPD members resigned in protest over the army's attack on the Marstall sailors. The result was the formation of volunteer units known as Free Corps (*Freikorps*).

The **Freikorps**

In 1918–19 something like 150 separate *Freikorps* were formed in Germany. They varied in size from over 10,000 men to fewer than 500. In 1919 total *Freikorps* strength was in excess of 250,000 men. Individual *Freikorps* were usually named after the officers who raised and commanded them. General von Hülsen's 11,000 strong *Freikorps Hülsen* was one of the largest units and Lieutenant-Commander Hermann Ehrhardt's *Marinebrigade Ehrhardt* probably the most notorious. Motives for joining a *Freikorps* were varied. Some *Freikorps* volunteers were straightforward mercenaries, attracted by relatively generous rates of pay. Others were motivated principally by anti-communism (see Figure 1). For the most part, however, the ethos of the *Freikorps* was right-wing, anti-socialist and anti-Semitic. *Freikorps* officers were often strongly pro-monarchist and therefore hostile in principle to the Republic they fought to defend in 1919–20. They defended it because they saw it as the lesser of two evils – the greater evil being a communist Germany.

The suppression of the Spartacists

It was *Freikorps* units that suppressed the Spartacist revolt in Berlin. Because the Spartacists were numerically weak and equipped only with light weapons, the task was not a demanding one in military terms. 'Spartacus week' (6–11 January 1919) was followed by a mopping-up operation in which the *Freikorps* showed themselves to be ruthless and vindictive. Their principal victims were Karl Liebknecht and Rosa Luxemburg. Arrested on 14 January, both were beaten and then shot on the orders of Captain Pabst of General Hoffman's

Garde-Kavallerie Schützen-Division. The murder of Liebknecht and Luxemburg had important political consequences. It poisoned relations between the KPD and the SPD – on whose behalf the *Freikorps* were acting in January 1919 – and helped to create an atmosphere in which throughout the Weimar period collaboration of any kind between the two parties was out of the question.

The Weimar constitution

Elections to the Constituent Assembly took place as scheduled on 19 January 1919. The SPD emerged as the largest single party with a 38% share of the vote and 163 of the 421 seats. It was, however, outnumbered by anti-socialist parties largely representing the middle and upper classes. The combined strength of these parties – the Nationalist Party (DNVP), the People's Party (DVP), the Democratic Party (DDP) and the Centre – was 249 seats, just over half the total. Germany's socialists no longer had a monopoly of political power.

The Assembly started work on 6 February 1919 – not at Berlin, still tense and disturbed, but at the small town of Weimar, 150 miles to the south-west. Here, guarded by 7,000 *Freikorps* troops, it was able to deliberate in safety. By 10 February agreement had been reached on an interim constitution, the purpose of which was to allow Ebert's government to be replaced by one whose authority was based on the democratic vote of 19 January. The agreement provided for a government, headed by a Chancellor, which would be accountable to the Assembly, together with a President with emergency powers. On 11 February the Assembly elected Ebert President. At the same time an SPD-Centre-Democratic Party coalition government was formed with the socialist Scheidemann at its head as Chancellor.

The Weimar constitution in its full and final form was approved by the Assembly on 31 July 1919. It owed much to the efforts of Hugo Preuss, a constitutional lawyer and a member of the liberal Democratic Party (*Deutsche Demokratische Partei* – DDP). The Constitution (see Figure 2) was a complex document consisting of no fewer than 181 separate articles. Essentially, though, there are three things about it which need to be remembered.

◆ The constitution established a federal system in which political authority was divided between individual states (*Länder*) and the central or federal government. The powers of the states, however, were relatively limited.

◆ The Weimar system of government was a hybrid affair based partly on the British-style parliamentary system and partly on the United States' system, with its directly-elected President. The expectation was that in normal circumstances Germany should be governed by ministers responsible to the Reichstag but under Article 48 of the constitution the President was given powers to intervene in an emergency. Between 1930 and 1933 Germany was governed continuously on the basis of these emergency powers. The framers of the Weimar constitution had not intended that Article 48 would be used in this way.

◆ The Reichstag was elected by proportional representation. It is sometimes claimed that this was an important cause of Weimar Germany's frequent changes of government in the 1920s. This is not true. Weimar Germany's political instability had far more to do with the fact that there were half a dozen political parties each capable of winning a sizeable share of the vote in Reichstag elections – meaning that governments could only be formed and could only survive if three or more parties were in agreement – than it had to do with proportional representation. Political instability would have been a problem in the 1920s whatever electoral system had been adopted.

Figure 2
The Weimar Constitution, 1919

The Reich Chancellor and the Reich Cabinet
The Reich Chancellor and Cabinet formed, under ordinary circumstances, the government of Germany. The Reich Chancellor presided over the government. The Reich Chancellor and the Reich ministers were under Article 54 of the constitution accountable to the Reichstag and had to resign if they lost the Reichstag's confidence.

The Reichstag
The lower, and more important, house of the legislature or law-making body.
Elected for four years at a time by proportional representation.

President
The President (*Reichspraesident*) was elected for seven years by the whole electorate. If no candidate in a presidential election won an absolute majority (i.e. over 50% of votes cast) on the first ballot, a second election took place in which the winner was the candidate who won the biggest share of the vote. The President was the head of state and commander-in-chief of the armed forces. Under Article 48 had emergency powers to suspend individual rights and take whatever measures were necessary to restore order.

Bill of Rights
The Weimar constitution contained clauses guaranteeing individual rights such as the freedom of speech, freedom of assembly and freedom of association.

The Reichsrat
The upper, and less important, house of the legislature. The Reichsrat represented the 17 *Länder* or states in the law making process. It could block, or undo laws passed by the Reichstag, but the latter could override a Reichsrat veto by passing a measure by a two-thirds majority. Each state had one vote in the Reichsrat for every 700,000 of its inhabitants. States were represented in the Reichsrat by members of their state governments.

State (or Land) Governments
There were 17 states or *Länder* in all:
Bavaria, Saxony, Württemburg, Baden, Thuringia, Hesse, Hamburg, Mecklenburg-Schwerin, Oldenburg, Brunswick, Anhalt, Bremen, Lippe, Lübeck, Waldeck, Schaumburg-Lippe and Prussia.

Each state or *Land* was responsible for its own educational and judicial system and for its own police service. Each state had its own law-making body or *Landtag* and each had its own government. Laws passed by the Reichstag prevailed over laws passed by a *Landtag* if the two were in conflict.

The Electorate
All Germans over the age of 20

The KPD after 1919

The suppression of the Spartacist revolt in 1919 deprived the KPD of its ablest leaders but it did not by any means end the threat to the Weimar Republic from the extreme left. Communist-inspired disorder and political violence was a continuing problem in later 1919 and in the early 1920s.

In January 1919 KPD risings in the North Sea ports of Cuxhaven, Wilhelmshaven and Bremen were bloodily put down by *Freikorps* troops. Two months later, in March, the KPD called a general strike in Berlin. Fighting broke out when *Freikorps* units moved out on to the streets. Eventually they crushed the strike at the cost of 1,500 dead and 10,000 wounded.

It was, however, the south German state of Bavaria which witnessed the worst *Freikorps* atrocities in 1919. In November 1918, following the Kiel mutiny, an independent socialist republic had been proclaimed in Bavaria. Its leader was the idealistic Kurt Eisner, a journalist and intellectual belonging to the USPD. Eisner remained in power until February 1919, when he was assassinated by Count Arco-Valley, a deranged right-wing extremist. After Eisner's death Bavaria shifted further to the left. In April 1919 it became a soviet republic under the leadership of two Russian-born Communists, Max Levien and Eugene Leviné. In May the infant republic was suppressed by a 35,000 strong *Freikorps* force. In the process 600 were killed. KPD morale was dented by its defeats but further risings were nevertheless attempted in the Ruhr (1920), Saxony (1923) and Hamburg (1923). In the mid-1920s the KPD regrouped under the leadership of Ernst Thälmann (1886–1944). Thälmann's KPD was closely linked with Stalin's Russia, more or less taking its orders from Moscow.

How serious was the threat from the left, 1918–23?

At the end of the First World War the KPD established control, albeit temporarily, over all or part of major cities like Berlin and Bremen and over the state of Bavaria. A political movement capable of doing this obviously cannot be written off as wholly inconsequential. The KPD was clearly a threat of some significance to the Weimar Republic in 1918–19. There were certainly several factors at work in its favour. By far the most important of these was the existence of working-class discontent off which it could feed. In 1918–19, to quote the British historian Elizabeth Wiskemann, "defeated armies returned to starving homes". Not surprisingly, Communist rallies and demonstrations during this period often attracted large audiences. Other factors working in the KPD's favour were the backing it received from Lenin's Russia and the unreliability of the rank-and-file of the army from the point of view of the authorities.

It would, however, be a mistake to overestimate the significance of the Communist threat. Germany was never in really serious danger of succumbing to Communism in 1918–19. There are several reasons why this is so.

◆ The KPD lacked popular support. The highest share of the vote it received in Reichstag elections of the 1920s was 12.6%. In 1918–19 workers may have attended its rallies but in general they showed little enthusiasm for the kind of political change it advocated. The researches of historians like Wolfgang Mommsen suggest that working-class protest in 1918–19 was motivated very largely by economic issues – food shortages and the like –

rather than by a desire for political upheaval. Germany's industrialists also acted shrewdly to take the sting out of working-class protest. Under the Legien–Stinnes agreement of November 1918 Germany's trades unions were offered an eight-hour day and other concessions in return for acceptance of the employers' property rights.

◆ The KPD was poorly led. It certainly had no-one who exhibited the kind of political insight and ruthlessness displayed by Lenin in Russia in 1917. Karl Liebknecht and Rosa Luxemburg did not control or direct the Spartacist rising to any great effect in early 1919. The rising was an ill-co-ordinated and botched affair.

◆ The Majority Socialist leaders were determined and resolute in their opposition to the revolutionaries. Ebert hated revolution 'like sin' and Noske had no scruples about backing the *Freikorps* in 1919 despite the atrocities they committed.

Studying 'The German Revolution 1918–19'

1 The German Revolution of 1918–19 is a complex topic. It is important to establish a chronological grasp of events. These have not been dealt with in this chapter in strict chronological order and constructing a time chart showing them is therefore a useful exercise. Your chart should include (at least) the following events: the 'revolution from above'; the Kiel mutiny; the proclamation of Eisner's socialist republic in Bavaria; the Kaiser's departure for Holland; the establishment of the Council of People's Commissars; the armistice; 'Spartacus week'; the murder of Liebknecht and Luxemburg; the Constituent Assembly elections; Ebert's election as President; the murder of Eisner; the suppression of the Bavarian Soviet Republic; approval of the final version of the Weimar constitution by the Constituent Assembly.

2 Another way of deepening your understanding of these events is to focus on the part played by individuals. Make notes (a short paragraph for each) on the role in the German Revolution of 1918–19 of the following: Prince Max of Baden; Friedrich Ebert; Wilhelm Groener; Gustav Noske; Kurt Eisner.

3 You will need to be able to explain why the extreme left failed to take power in Germany in 1918–19. Make notes (a paragraph each or a flow chart) on the importance in this connection of each of the following: lack of popular support; poor leadership; the strength and determination of the opposition.

4 It is not easy to fix the precise date on which the Weimar Republic was established. Explain what can be said for and against each of the following as a date for the formation of the Weimar Republic:

9 November 1918; 19 December 1918; 10 February 1919; 31 July 1919.

3 The threat from the right, 1919–23

How serious was the threat from extreme right-wing groups to the survival of the Weimar Republic?

Key points

◆ Who were the parties and paramilitaries of the extreme right?
◆ The extreme right was a more serious danger than the extreme left in the early 1920s and used violence to oppose the Republic
◆ The extreme right hated the Treaty of Versailles and blamed the Republic for it
◆ How serious was the threat from the right, 1919–23?

'The enemies of the state stand on the right.' This declaration was made in the Reichstag in 1922 by Joseph Wirth, then Chancellor, following the assassination of Walter Rathenau, his Foreign Minister, by right-wing terrorists. It is certainly true that in the early 1920s the extreme right posed a more serious threat to the Weimar Republic than did the extreme left. The extreme right had deeper roots in German society than the extreme left and in the early 1920s events moved in its favour.

Who were the political parties and paramilitaries of the extreme right?

The DNVP

The extreme right in the early years of the Weimar Republic was not a unified and coherent political movement. Instead there was a multiplicity of extreme right-wing parties and groupings. The most important political party of the extreme right in the early to mid-1920s was the German Nationalist People's Party (the *Deutschnationale Volkspartei*, or DNVP). The DNVP was essentially the party of the *Junkers* and of big business, but it also had middle-class and even working-class supporters. In policy terms, the DNVP was monarchist and authoritarian. Under its first leader, Karl Helfferich, it opted for the political sidelines, avoiding any involvement in government while subjecting the infant Republic to a barrage of abuse.

In the mid-1920s, under the less extreme leadership of Count Westarp, there was a change in tactics: on two occasions (in 1925 and 1927), the DNVP entered government with the purpose of protecting the interests of landowners and capitalists. In 1928, however, Westarp was ousted from the leadership by the media tycoon and hardliner, Alfred Hugenberg. Under Hugenberg's leadership the DNVP reverted to Helfferich's policy of cold-shouldering the Republic.

The Nazis

The Nazi Party (*Nationalsozialistische Deutsche Arbeiterpartei*, or NSDAP) was founded in 1920. In many respects its doctrines differed little from those of the DNVP: it was anti-Republican, anti-Communist, anti-democratic, anti-Versailles and ultra-nationalistic. The Nazis, though, were never a monarchist party and their racism and anti-Semitism were probably more obsessive and hysterical than anything to be found in the DNVP. In the early 1920s, the Nazis were a force in the politics of the state of Bavaria, but were not a major force in national politics. This was not to change until later in the 1920s.

Paramilitary groups

Immediately after the war it was the paramilitary *Freikorps* rather than the DNVP or Nazis who were the main standard-bearers of the extreme right. Their ascendancy, though, was short-lived. In 1920, following the imposition of restrictions on the size of Germany's army by the Treaty of Versailles, the *Freikorps* were either disbanded or incorporated into the regular army.

Other paramilitary groups such as the *Stahlhelm* and the *Jungdo* soon rose to prominence in their place. The *Stahlhelm* ('steel helmets'), nominally an ex-servicemen's organisation, was founded in 1918 by Franz Seldte, subsequently Nazi Minister of Labour. Its membership increased sharply in the early 1920s, eventually reaching 400,000. In the later 1920s it effectively became the DNVP's private army. The anti-Semitic *Jungdo* ('Young German Order'), formed in 1920, almost equalled the *Stahlhelm* in size.

The *Sturmabteilung* (SA), the paramilitary wing of Hitler's Nazi Party, acquired a reputation for brutality in the later 1920s which neither the *Stahlhelm* nor the *Jungdo* could match.

The strength of the extreme right

The strength of the extreme right lay not only in political parties and paramilitary groups but also in the extent to which its supporters were entrenched in key positions in German society. The most powerful institution in which monarchist and anti-Republican sentiments were rife was the German army, known after 1919 as the *Reichswehr*. The *Reichswehr* did not actively seek to overthrow the Republic in the 1920s, but neither did it do much to support it. The historian Helmut Heiber describes the *Reichswehr*'s attitude to the Weimar Republic as one of 'contemptuous loyalty'.

Other institutions with a strongly anti-Republican ethos were the judiciary, the police, the universities, secondary schools and, to a lesser extent, the civil service. Indicative of attitudes within them was the reply of Ernst Pohner, Munich's police chief, when a democratic politician told him that right-wing murder gangs were active in Bavaria: "I know – but not enough of them."

The Treaty of Versailles and right-wing hatred of the Republic

The formation of the Weimar Republic deprived the extreme right of much of its power and influence. It was also the case that the new Republic appeared to extreme right-wingers to be dominated by those they most despised: liberals, socialists, Catholics and Jews. They called it a *Sozi-Republik* (socialist republic) or a *Kommunist Judenrepublik* (Communist-Jewish republic). These are two of the reasons why right-wing hostility to the Republic was so deep and enduring. A third reason was the peace settlement.

To the extreme right the peace settlement was a *Schmachfrieden* (shameful peace) for which the Weimar Republic was unquestionably to blame. After 1919 democratic politicians who had agreed to the armistice in 1918 were persistently derided by the extreme right as the 'November Criminals'. The extreme right also claimed throughout the 1920s that Germany's armies had not been defeated in the war but in 1918 had been betrayed, or stabbed in the back, by Republican politicians when they had been capable of fighting on. This claim, entirely false, is known as the *Dolchstosslegende* ('stab-in-the-back myth').

When the Allies' peace terms were published in May 1919 they were condemned not only by the extreme right, but by all shades of political opinion in Germany. Scheidemann's SPD-Centre Party-Democratic Party coalition government even considered restarting the war rather than accept them. Extreme right-wingers, however, condemned the terms – and the Versailles Treaty in which they were embodied in June 1919 – more ferociously than anyone (see Figure 3 for the Treaty's main terms). They also sought throughout the 1920s to exploit popular indignation over the Treaty in order to undermine the Republic.

There was a great deal in the 440 articles of the Versailles Treaty that the extreme right regarded as abhorrent. Three aspects of the Treaty, though, aroused especial bitterness:

◆ There was objection not only to the terms of the Treaty but to the manner in which it was made. When Germany agreed to the armistice, it was assumed that there would be negotiations with the Allies. It was further assumed that these negotiations would take place on the basis of Woodrow Wilson's Fourteen Points. These were proposals for a peace without annexations which had been put forward by the US President Wilson in January 1918 – that is, when the stalemate on the Western Front had not yet been broken. In the event the Fourteen Points were largely ignored, and there were no negotiations: the Allies first gave the German delegation in Paris three weeks to make 'observations' on the terms and then, on 16 June, insisted on acceptance of them within five days. The Germans maintained they had been unjustly treated. The Versailles Treaty was branded a *Diktat* – a dictated peace.

◆ The loss of territory to Poland was deeply resented. In large part this was because the Poles were viewed by the extreme right as *Lausevolk* ('lice people'), backward and primitive, but there were other reasons too. First, over a million Germans found themselves under Polish control without being given a say in the matter. This appeared to Germans to be at odds with the principle of national self-determination in which the Allies said they believed and which they put into practice elsewhere. Second, East Prussia was cut off from the remainder of Germany.

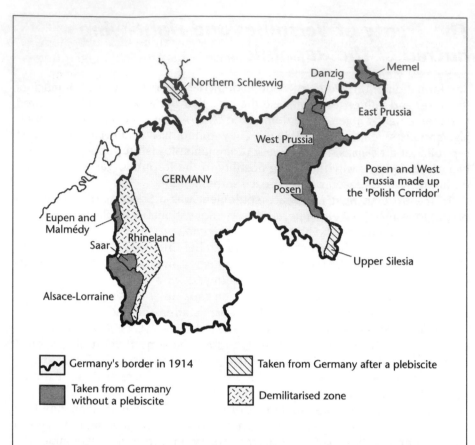

Figure 3
The main features of the
Treaty of Versailles, 1919

Territorial provisions

◆ GERMANY'S LOSSES WITHOUT A PLEBISCITE: **Alsace-Lorraine** (to France); **Eupen** and **Malmédy**
(to Belgium); **Posen** and **West Prussia** (to Poland); the city of **Danzig** (became as free
city under League of Nations control); **Memel** (occupied by France but ceded to
Lithuania, 1923)
◆ GERMANY'S LOSSES FOLLOWING A PLEBISCITE: **North Schleswig** (to Denmark); **Upper Silesia**
(to Poland)
◆ The **Rhineland** became a demilitarised zone, with the west (or left) bank to be occupied
by Allied forces for 15 years
◆ The **Saar** was placed under League of Nations control for 15 years, during which time its
coal mines were to be under French administration; after 15 years a plebiscite to be held
to determine its future
◆ **Anschluss**, or union between Austria and Germany, was forbidden by Article 80 of the
Treaty

German colonial losses

All colonies were to be forfeited, notably **German East Africa** (became a British mandate
under the League of Nations); **German South-West Africa** (became a South African
mandate); **Togoland** and **Cameroon** (joint Anglo-French mandate) and **Samoa** (New
Zealand mandate)

Military conditions

◆ German army to be restricted to **100,00 men; no conscription, no tanks or heavy
artillery; no general staff**
◆ German navy restricted to **15,000 men; no submarines**; German fleet limited to
six battleships (of less than 100,000 tonnes), six cruisers and 12 destroyers
◆ Germany not to be permitted an **air force**

Reparations

◆ Article 231 of the Treaty (the 'war guilt' clause) held Germany responsible for all 'loss and
damage' suffered by the Allies during the war and provided the basis for reparations
◆ The total sum due was not fixed in 1919 but was to be decided by an Inter-Allied
Reparations Commission (which reported in 1921 and fixed Germany's liability at
£6,600,000 or 132 billion marks)

◆ The reparations provisions were condemned as unjustifiable. In German eyes, the Allies' proposals had no foundation in either legality or morality. The basis of the Allies' reparations demands was Article 231 of the Treaty – the 'war guilt' clause – which Germany was forced to accept. Germans however, denied they alone bore responsibility for the war. The 'war-guilt lie' became a favourite target of the extreme right. It was, moreover, clear even before the Reparations Commission reported In 1921 that Germany's reparations liability was likely to be beyond its capacity to pay. In 1919 the Allies made it clear that the cost of war pensions as well as physical damage would be included in the reparations bill and they demanded an immediate £1,000 million payment on account. The extreme right claimed that the Allies' aim was to turn Germany into what one of its newspapers called an 'economic corpse'.

Violent opposition

The Kapp Putsch, 1920

The word '*putsch*' literally means a thrust or blow. In political terms a 'putsch' is an attempt to seize power. The Kapp Putsch – or more accurately the Kapp-Lüttwitz Putsch – was an extreme right-wing attempt to overthrow the Weimar Republic which resulted directly from the imposition of the Treaty of Versailles.

In early 1919 the strength of the *Reichswehr*, the regular army, was estimated at 350,000. There were in addition in excess of 250,000 men enlisted in the various *Freikorps*. Under the terms of the Versailles Treaty, Germany was required to reduce its armed forces to a maximum of 100,000. *Freikorps* units therefore had to be disbanded.

In March 1920 orders were issued for the disbandment of the *Marinebrigade Ehrhardt*. Its leaders were determined to resist dissolution and appealed to General Lüttwitz, commander of the Berlin *Reichswehr*, for support. Lüttwitz, an organiser of *Freikorps* units in 1918–19 and a fervent monarchist, responded by calling on Ebert and Noske to stop the whole programme of troop reductions. When Ebert refused, Lüttwitz ordered the *Marinebrigade Ehrhardt* to march on

Figure 4
Translation of the government proclamation, 1920

WORKERS! PARTY COMRADES!

The military putsch is here! The Freebooters who were afraid they would be dissolved have made an attempt to overthrow the Republic and establish a dictatorial government with Kapp and Lüttwitz at its head.

WORKERS! COMRADES!

We did not make a revolution only to have it overthrown by a bloody Freebooter regiment.

THEREFORE STOP WORK! STRIKE!

Throttle the reactionary clique. Fight with every means for the maintenance of the Republic. Lay aside all petty disagreement. There is only one way to prevent the return of Wilhelm II:

PARALYSE ALL ECONOMIC ACTIVITY!
NO HAND DARE MOVE!
NO WORKER DARE HELP THE MILITARY DICTATORSHIP!
GENERAL STRIKE ALL DOWN THE LINE!

WORKERS UNITE! DOWN WITH THE COUNTER REVOLUTION!

Berlin. It occupied the capital on 13 March. Lüttwitz, therefore, was the driving force behind the 1920 putsch. Its nominal leader, though, was Wolfgang Kapp, a 62-year-old East Prussian civil servant and rabid nationalist.

At this point Noske, the defence minister, called upon the regular army to suppress the putsch. He encountered a blank refusal. General von Seeckt, one of the *Reichswehr*'s senior commanders, told him: "*Reichswehr* does not shoot on *Reichswehr*". The government, forced to abandon Berlin, moved to Stuttgart. As it did so it issued a proclamation calling on Germany's workers to defeat the putsch by means of a general strike (Figure 4). The strike call received massive support. With the country paralysed, the putsch collapsed. Kapp and Lüttwitz, unable to govern, fled to Sweden.

There were two main reasons why the Weimar Republic survived in 1920. First, the working class rallied to its defence. Second, Kapp and Lüttwitz had the support of only a minority of the extreme right. Many potential sympathisers, including most of the leading *Freikorps* commanders, thought the putsch ill-timed and refused to join it.

Organisation Consul

The *Marinebrigade Ehrhardt* was dissolved after the Kapp Putsch, but its most fanatical members now turned to assassination as a means of destabilising the Republic. They formed themselves into Organisation Consul, one of a number of right-wing death squads which in 1921–22 were responsible for over 350 killings. Organisation Consul's principal victims were the Centre Party leader and 'November Criminal' Matthias Erzberger (August 1921) and Walter Rathenau (June 1922). Organisation Consul was swept away in the storm of protest which followed the murder of Rathenau.

The occupation of the Ruhr, 1923

The Ruhr was Germany's most important heavy industrial region. In 1923 it was occupied by 100,000 French troops. The term 'occupation' is used to describe this episode rather than 'invasion' simply because France's troops encountered no resistance. Germany was powerless to resist by force because its army had been neutered by the Versailles Treaty.

France's occupation of the Ruhr resulted from its dissatisfaction with the Treaty of Versailles. At the Paris Peace Conference in 1919 France had wanted to partition Germany, thereby weakening it permanently, and had called for the Rhineland to be detached from the remainder of the country to form a separate state. Britain and the USA had overruled this proposal, offering the French instead a guarantee of support if they ever again became victims of German aggression. However, the Anglo-American guarantee lapsed in 1920 when the US Senate failed to ratify the Versailles Treaty. France therefore opted for a policy of rigid enforcement of the treaty, hoping in this way to keep Germany permanently weak.

In January 1923 a minor German default on reparations payments – non-delivery of a consignment of timber – gave the French an opportunity for harsh retribution. Their aim in occupying the Ruhr was to strip Germany of its wealth and strength. In addition, they may have hoped to remain in the Ruhr on a long-term basis, thus permanently depriving Germany of its heavy industrial base.

Hyperinflation

Unable to take military action against France, the German government – a DDP-Centre Party-People's Party coalition headed by Wilhelm Cuno, a non-party businessman – resorted to passive resistance. Workers, businessmen and civil servants were instructed not to co-operate in any way with the occupying forces. They were in effect called out on strike. Those who obeyed the strike call were to be compensated for their loss of income by payments from public funds. This policy of passive resistance involved a massive increase in the government's spending at a time when its income from taxation was reduced because the Ruhr was paralysed. Cuno's government covered this yawning gap between income and expenditure simply by printing money.

Germany was experiencing acute inflationary problems even before the occupation of the Ruhr. The Kaiser's government had financed the 1914–18 war not through taxation but by borrowing, the assumption being that Germany would win the war and would be able to repay its debts by forcing reparations out of the countries it had defeated. When this assumption proved false, confidence in Germany's currency, the mark, was badly dented. The value of the mark in relation of foreign currencies fell: the cost of imports of food and raw materials rose. Confidence in the mark declined further when the Allied Reparations Commission reported in 1921. This gave a twist to the inflationary spiral which had already begun.

By printing money on a massive scale in 1923 the Cuno government destroyed what confidence in the mark remained. The result was hyperinflation or 'currency delirium' (Helmut Heiber). In January 1923 one US dollar bought 10,000 marks; by September it bought 98 million marks. The mark declined significantly on a daily, even hourly, basis. In autumn 1923 Germany's money-based economy finally broke down completely and people turned to bartering goods.

The impact of hyperinflation within Germany was uneven. Some profited from it. Adroit speculators like the tycoon Hugo Stinnes made fortunes, and industrialists and landowners who owed money were able to pay off their debts in devalued currency. Others were able to escape the worst – those, for example, whose wealth took the form of property or those with goods or skills which could be readily bartered. Initially the working class suffered comparatively little because trade unions ensured that wages kept pace with rising prices, but as 1923 wore on their position deteriorated. The principal losers in 1923, though, were those with cash savings, many but not all of whom were in the middle class (the *Mittelstand*). Middle-class savers experienced the trauma of seeing the value of their savings completely wiped out.

The policy of passive resistance was unsustainable. Apart from the economic pain it caused it gave rise to widespread disorder. There was rioting and looting as food became scarce and a wave of strikes occurred in protest against rising prices. In August the Cuno government resigned to make way for a 'grand coalition' (SDP-DDP-Centre Party-People's Party) headed by Gustav Stresemann. Soon afterwards Stresemann called off passive resistance, despite receiving no assurance from the French that they would leave the Ruhr in return.

The Beer Hall Putsch 1923

The French entry into the Ruhr gave rise to feelings of intense nationalism in Germany. German opinion was further inflamed in the course of 1923 by acts of brutality committed by the occupying forces, notably the shooting of 13 Krupps workers in March and the execution of the ex-*Freikorps* fighter Albert Leo Schlageter for sabotage in May.

As ultra-nationalists and savage critics of the Versailles Treaty, extreme right-wingers were well placed to gain from the mood of anger and bitterness. Right-wing extremists were also able to make political capital out of Stresemann's abandonment of passive resistance with the French still in the Ruhr: they depicted the pro-Weimar politicians of the 'grand coalition' as cowards who had betrayed their country. With events apparently moving in their direction, right-wingers not surprisingly began to think in terms of a putsch.

In late 1923 a right-wing plot to overthrow the Republic began to take shape in Bavaria. The chief plotters were Gustav von Kahr, Bavaria's state commissioner and a fervent monarchist; Otto von Lossow, the local *Reichswehr* commander; and Colonel von Seisser, chief of the provincial police force. Their plan was to seize control of Bavaria and then march on Berlin. The plotters were well-connected. Among those aware of, and sympathetic to, their plans were General von Seeckt, head of the *Reichswehr*, the industrialist Hugo Stinnes and the former army chief Ludendorff. Also involved was Hitler's NSDAP.

By November Hitler had whipped up his followers into a fever pitch of excitement and was desperate to press ahead. Kahr, however, hesitated. Hitler decided to force him to act. On 8 November, Kahr, with Lossow and Seisser present, was addressing a meeting in one of Munich's beer halls. Hitler, who had moved SA units into the city, burst into the hall and declared that a putsch was under way. Kahr and the others were forced at gunpoint to declare their support for it. Having done so, they were allowed to slip away. Once free, they set about thwarting Hitler. On the following day, 9 November, forces loyal to Kahr were out on Munich's streets. Rather than accept defeat, Hitler, backed by Ludendorff, ordered his 3,000 SA men to march on the city's main army barracks, hoping to win over the local *Reichswehr*. At the Feldherrenhalle, the marchers encountered a police barricade. Firing started. Sixteen Nazis were killed. The rest fled. A right-wing putsch had been suppressed by other right-wingers without any intervention from forces loyal to the Republic.

After the Beer Hall Putsch, Ludendorff and Hitler stood trial for treason. Ludendorff, extraordinarily, was acquitted. Hitler was sentenced to five years' imprisonment, of which he served only one. Hitler's sentence was typical of the derisory punishments meted out by the predominantly anti-Weimar judiciary to extreme right-wing political offenders. What was perhaps untypical about Hitler's case was that he was brought to trial at all. Hostility to the Republic within Germany's police forces ensured that most right-wing thugs and murderers in the early 1920s escaped scot free.

How serious was the threat from the right in the early 1920s?

At the end of 1918 the extreme right looked discredited. The war it had done much to bring about had ended in national humiliation. The Kaiser had been forced to abdicate. In the 1919 Constituent Assembly election the DNVP was able to win only a fraction over 10% of votes cast. In the years after 1918, however, the extreme right made a remarkable political comeback. In the 1924 election the DNVP won over 19% of votes cast and the NSDAP won over 6%. In other words, more than a quarter of the electorate voted for one or other of the parties of the extreme right. The extreme right was able to feed off the resentment created in Germany by the Versailles Treaty, by the festering sore of reparations and by the Ruhr occupation. This was one reason for its recovery. Another was the willingness of some voters to believe its lies and slanders, notably the *Dolchstosslegende*.

The extreme right, then, was a formidable threat to the Weimar Republic in the early 1920s. It had a sizeable electoral base, extensive support within Germany's élites and – because of its paramilitary groups and *Reichswehr* links – considerable military potential. It was not, however, able to overthrow the Republic. There were three main reasons why this was so:

◆ Though it had a significant amount of popular support, the extreme right did not have majority support.

◆ The extreme right was weakened by internal divisions. There were tensions of various kinds – between civilian politicians and paramilitaries who despised civilians; between different *Freikorps* leaders; between *Reichswehr* and the *Freikorps*, the latter being seen by the former as anarchic and undisciplined; and between the DNVP and the NSDAP, at odds among other things over the issue of the restoration of the monarchy. Internal divisions were a significant factor in the failure of both the 1920 and 1923 putsch attempts.

◆ The Republic's supporters were prepared to defend it vigorously. This was evident not only in 1920 when the Kapp Putsch was defeated by a general strike, but also in 1922 when 700,000 people took to the streets of Berlin in protest at Rathenau's murder.

Studying 'The threat from the right, 1919–23'

1 There are a number of terms you need to understand. Write one or two sentences explaining the meaning of each of the following: monarchist; 'November Criminals'; *Diktat*; the 'war-guilt lie'; the *Dolchstosslegende*; putsch; hyperinflation; passive resistance.

2 You need to understand why the extreme right hated the Republic and why it failed to overthrow the Republic in 1919–23.

a) Identify, and briefly explain, three distinct reasons for the extreme right's hostility to the Weimar Republic.

b) On the basis of this chapter, make notes that summarise the strengths and weaknesses of the extreme right in 1919–23.

3 Explain, in three or four sentences each, the role and significance of the following as enemies of the Weimar Republic in 1919–23: Hermann Ehrhardt; General Lüttwitz; General von Seeckt; Otto von Kahr; Adolf Hitler.

4 What arguments do you think might have been made in the 1920s *against* the view that Germany had been very harshly treated under the Treaty of Versailles?

5 In note form, summarise **(a)** the causes and **(b)** the impact of hyperinflation on different social classes in Germany. How accurate is it to say that the middle classes were ruined by the events of 1923?

4 The 'golden years' of the Weimar Republic, 1924–29

How 'golden' were the middle years of the Weimar Republic?

Key points

- ◆ Between 1924 and 1929 Weimar Germany enjoyed a period of relative stability
- ◆ Stresemann's diplomacy was instrumental in bringing this about
- ◆ Deep-seated problems remained – economic weaknesses, political instability and political violence

---

The mid- to late 1920s are sometimes described as the 'golden years' of the Weimar Republic. In some ways it is an appropriate term. Between 1924 and 1929 Germany's international standing improved; a measure of economic recovery took place; the social welfare system was strengthened; the arts flourished; and there were no putsch attempts. On the other hand, the problems of political instability and paramilitary violence did not go away and serious conflicts occurred between employers and unions. In addition, an avowed monarchist was elected President. For these reasons some historians use the term 'relative stabilisation' rather than 'golden years' to describe the years 1924–29.

The role of Gustav Stresemann

Stresemann's Chancellorship

Gustav Stresemann was the son of a Berlin publican who enjoyed a successful academic and business career before entering the Reichstag in 1907. As a young politician he was noted for the virulence of his right-wing views. In 1918 Stresemann co-founded the People's Party (*Deutsche Volkspartei*, or DVP). The DVP became the party of small and medium-size business interests and of the managerial classes. Originally it was monarchist, viewing the Republic with disdain, but in the early 1920s opinion within it shifted in favour of making the Republic work. Stresemann, appalled by the murders of Erzberger and Rathenau, and leaving his extremist past behind him, was instrumental in bringing about this change of attitude. There was, though, an element within the DVP which never reconciled itself to the Republic and after Stresemann's death the party lurched to the right.

Stresemann served as Chancellor for a mere 103 days in August–November 1923. In that time, however, he did much to ensure that the Republic emerged intact from the crisis threatening to engulf it. After calling off passive resistance, he proceeded to stabilise the currency, overseeing in November the introduction of a new currency, the Rentenmark, which unlike its predecessor was issued in strictly limited quantities. He also acted decisively to forestall a threatened Communist rising in Saxony and refused to be panicked by the activities of the extreme right in Bavaria. Stresemann by his conduct in late 1923 made enemies on both left and right and it was this which cost him the Chancellorship. He went on, however, to serve continuously as foreign minister until his death in 1929.

Stresemann's foreign policy

Stresemann's foreign policy was built around the concept of *Erfüllungspolitik* or 'fulfilment'. He was not, though, the originator of the policy of 'fulfilment'. It had been initiated by Wirth and Rathenau in 1921–22. In essence, 'fulfilment' was an attempt to improve relations with Britain and France by complying with the terms of the Versailles Treaty, it being assumed that the two Western powers, once convinced of Germany's good intentions, would be willing to modify or revise the treaty. Stresemann practised 'fulfilment' to considerable effect. Between 1924 and 1929 Germany's international position was transformed. "We were a people of helots [slaves], and today we are once more a state of world consequence", was the judgement of one of his ministerial colleagues, Hans Luther. Stresemann's success owed much to his own negotiating skill, but other factors were at work too. After 1924 France abandoned the hardline policy which had led to the Ruhr occupation and instead sought security against German attack through reconciliation. In addition, Britain and France feared that unless concessions were offered to Germany it might be driven into the arms of the Soviet Union.

Stresemann's diplomacy in the mid- to late 1920s contributed to a series of international agreements from which Germany benefited substantially.

◆ In 1924 French troops withdrew from the Ruhr on the basis of the Dawes Plan. Named after the American banker who helped draft it, the Dawes Plan put the payment of reparations on to a new footing. Under it, Germany's total liability remained unchanged but annual payments were reduced. There were other benefits for Germany in the Dawes Plan: the Allies undertook not to occupy German cities in the event of non-payment of debts, and a sizeable loan (200 million dollars) was arranged to boost Germany's financial reserves. These benefits, though, came at a price: security for the loan had to be given in the shape of the assets of the German railway system, and Germany had to accept a measure of foreign control over its national bank.

◆ In 1925 the Locarno Pact was agreed. Under the Pact, Germany, France and Belgium pledged themselves not to use force to change the borders laid down in the Versailles Treaty. What this meant in practice was that Germany abandoned any claim to Alsace-Lorraine and France undertook not to repeat its occupation of the Ruhr. On balance, since regaining Alsace-Lorraine was a very long way from the top of any German agenda, Germany gained more out of Locarno than it conceded.

The Locarno Pact gave rise to a great deal of optimism that the historic quarrel between France and Germany had finally been buried. Not surprisingly, Stresemann and his French opposite number, Aristide Briand, were in 1926 jointly awarded the Nobel Peace prize. In the later 1920s there was much talk of 'the spirit of Locarno'. A manifestation of it was the Pact of Paris (1928), in which 60 nations solemnly (and meaninglessly) agreed to renounce war as an instrument of national policy.

◆ In 1925 the Allies agreed to remove their occupation forces from the Cologne area. In 1926 they agreed to withdraw the Inter-Allied Military Control Commission (the function of which was to monitor German compliance with the military clauses of the Versailles treaty) from Germany and to reduce the number of occupying troops to 60,000. In 1929 they agreed to remove all remaining occupying forces from the Rhineland by 1930, five years ahead of schedule.

◆ In 1926, in accordance with an understanding reached at Locarno, Germany became a member of the League of Nations with a permanent seat on its Council. The other permanent members of the League's Council were Britain, France, Italy and Japan. In practical terms, Germany's entry into the League meant little but it was of symbolic importance: it showed that Germany was no longer an outcast from the international community.

◆ In 1929 Stresemann agreed to the Young Plan, which took its name from the American financier who chaired negotiations between Germany and the Allies. The Young Plan replaced the stop-gap Dawes Plan and was intended to be a final settlement of the reparations issue. Under it Germany's total reparations liability was reduced from the 132 billion marks demanded in 1921 to 37 billion marks. There were to be 58 annual repayments, the last falling due in 1988. The foreign controls over the German economy contained within the Dawes Plan were ended. In the event, the Young Plan was not operative for long. Against a background of economic depression and financial crisis, the Allies first allowed Germany to suspend repayments (1931) and then to discontinue them altogether (1932).

Stresemann was not a sentimentalist who believed in international reconciliation for its own sake but was a hard-headed champion of Germany's national interests. At heart he remained a German nationalist. Through 'fulfilment' he hoped eventually to remove the reparations burden in its entirety, to regain the territory lost to Poland, to bring about *Anschluss* (Austro-German union) and to re-establish Germany's military strength – in short, to restore German power in Europe in full.

Successful though it was by any objective measure, Stresemann's diplomacy earned him nothing but hatred from the extreme right. During the years 1923–29 he was subjected to a vicious campaign of vilification. To the extreme right, the abandonment of passive resistance amounted to treason and agreement to the Dawes Plan entailed acceptance of the 'war-guilt lie'. It was also claimed that the foreign controls over the economy introduced under the Dawes Plan meant the 'enslavement' of Germany. The right's anti-Stresemann campaign culminated in a joint DNVP-*Stahlhelm*-Nazi attack on the Young Plan. Its orchestrator was Alfred Hugenberg. Claiming that the Young Plan further 'enslaved' Germany by committing generations as yet unborn to the payment of unjustifiable claims, Hugenberg and his associates forced a referendum on the issue of whether or not it should be accepted. When the referendum was held in December 1929 they won the support of only 5.8 million voters, far short of the 21 million needed for success. By this time, however, Stresemann had been dead for more than two months (see Figure 5).

Figure 5
Cartoon from *Vorwärts*, the SPD newspaper, 1929. The Nazis and Nationalists following Hugenberg are carrying a stink bomb, a bucket of manure and placards saying "Traitor" and "Stresemann, rot in hell". The nurse is saying "You're too late, he's already dead." The caption of the cartoon is "Their quarry has escaped them".

The economy in the 'golden years'

In the mid- to late 1920s Germany had a stable currency, competitive interest rates and an increasingly settled place within the international community. As a result it became a magnet for foreign investment. Between 1924 and 1930 nearly 5 billion dollars was invested in Germany from abroad, much of it from the United States. Fuelled by foreign funds, the German economy grew, though it did so erratically and comparatively slowly. In 1928 industrial production exceeded pre-war levels. Export performance was also strong: in 1929 exports were 40% higher than they had been in 1925.

The working classes were perhaps the chief beneficiaries of the increased prosperity of the later 1920s. Aided by state-sponsored compulsory arbitration schemes, trades unions succeeded in winning significant increases in real wages. The working classes benefited too from increased social welfare spending. The 1927 Labour Exchanges and Unemployment Insurance Act introduced an elaborate scheme of unemployment insurance, financed by employers, workers and the state, which complemented the generous pensions and sickness insurance scheme introduced under Bismarck in the 1880s. The later 1920s also saw a dramatic improvement in Germany's housing stock as local authorities took advantage of the ready availability of loans to embark on vast public housing schemes.

A measure of prosperity there may have been, but there was no 'economic miracle' in the later 1920s to compare with the one which transformed West Germany in the 1950s. In a number of respects the Weimar economy was structurally unsound.

♦ Prosperity was heavily dependent on foreign investment, much of which took the form of loans and credits which could be withdrawn at short notice.

♦ Governments in the late 1920s lived beyond their means. Public spending was significantly higher than income from taxation. The gap between the two – the budget deficit – was made up by borrowing. This state of affairs could not persist indefinitely.

♦ Export performance, though strong, was accompanied by a surge in imports. In 1927–28 Germany was importing more than it was exporting. There was, in other words, a trade deficit.

♦ Unemployment was higher in the later 1920s than it had been in the early 1920s. One reason for this was the success of trades unions in winning wage increases for their members. Employers reacted by trying wherever possible to cut labour costs. This frequently meant laying workers off. It also involved attempts by employers to resist the unions' wage demands. In 1928, for example, over 250,000 workers in the Ruhr steel industry were locked out by employers intent on blocking a wage rise. Similar disputes occurred elsewhere.

♦ Agriculture was an economic blackspot. Agricultural prices fell in the later 1920s and as a result farmers were often faced with mounting debts.

It was not only Germany's farmers but also the *Mittelstand* – small businessmen, lower middle-class white collar workers and the like – who largely missed out on the relative prosperity of the later 1920s. Having borne the brunt of hyper-inflation in 1923, members of the *Mittelstand* now felt that they were losing ground to the working classes in terms of income and status. This left them embittered and resentful. There were complaints that Weimar Germany was nothing but a 'trade union state'. Even in the 'golden years' the tensions in German society were acute.

Weimar culture

"In the richness and variety of its cultural accomplishments", states Gordon Craig (*Germany 1866–1945*, 1981), "the Weimar period is second to none in German history." There was certainly a dazzling array of talent at work. In literature there was Thomas Mann, Nobel Prize winner in 1929; Franz Kafka, author of *The Trial* (1925), Czech-born but a writer in German and a resident of Berlin; Erich Maria Remarque, author of the anti-war novel *All Quiet on the Western Front* (1927); and the left-wing dramatists Bertolt Brecht, Erwin Piscator and Ernst Toller. The political left was also to the fore in the visual arts in the shape of George Grosz, John Heartfield (born Helmut Herzfeld), Otto Dix, Max Ernst and Käthe Kollwitz. Leading figures in the world of music were Richard Strauss, Alban Berg, Paul Hindemith and Kurt Weill. Out of the German cinema there emerged classics such as *The Cabinet of Dr Caligari* (1919), a pioneer horror film, Fritz Lang's *Metropolis* (1927) and Joseph von Sternberg's *The Blue Angel* (1930), starring Marlene Dietrich. In the field of architecture and design, Walter Gropius founded the Bauhaus (House for the Building Arts) in 1919 to break down the barrier between art and craftsmanship. It became renowned for designs which were simple and functional yet elegant. Teachers at the

Bauhaus included the artists Wassily Kandinsky, Paul Klee and Oskar Kokoschka.

Glittering though Weimar culture was, it did little to generate support for the Republic. Artists and writers like Grosz, Heartfield and Toller were KPD sympathisers and were anti-Weimar. They may have attacked the Nazis in their work but they attacked Republican targets too. Grosz, for example, produced savage caricatures of Friedrich Ebert as well as of Hitler. Weimar culture also provided the extreme right with another stick with which to beat the Republic. The Nazis and the DNVP maintained that the outburst of experimentation in the arts was not something to be welcomed but was instead a symptom of decadence and decline. In the later 1920s right-wing extremists campaigned energetically against what they claimed was the tide of 'filth' and 'rubbish' which was sweeping across the country.

Political instability and electoral trends

Governments were no more durable after 1924 than they had been previously. In the five years between February 1919 and November 1923 nine separate governments held office. Their average lifespan was six and a half months. In the four and a half years between November 1923 and June 1928 there were six governments which on average survived for just over nine months. The principal obstacles in the way of stable government remained the same throughout the Weimar period: parties like the KPD, NSDAP and (for the most part) the DNVP refused to take part in the work of running the country and the predominantly working-class SPD, between 1919 and 1932 the largest single party in the Reichstag, was in general reluctant to join the middle-class pro-Weimar parties in government. In these circumstances the burden of government fell on the DVP, the Democrats and the Centre Party which between them came nowhere near commanding a majority of the Reichstag.

If political instability remained a problem, pro-Weimar elements were able in the later 1920s to take some comfort from electoral trends. In the two elections of 1924, held in the aftermath of the Ruhr occupation, the right-wing parties had predictably made gains. In 1928, however, both the DNVP and the Nazi vote declined. Prosperity, however unevenly spread, appears to have diminished the appeal of extremism.

Hindenburg's election to the Presidency

In 1925 President Ebert died suddenly at the age of 56. The presidential election which followed saw each of the main parties fielding its own candidate, none of whom came close to winning the required overall majority. A second ballot was therefore necessary. This time the 78-year-old Paul von Hindenburg, wartime head of the army High Command and one of the architects of the 'revolution from above' in 1918, was persuaded to enter the fray as the candidate of the DNVP and the DVP. He proceeded to win a narrow victory over Wilhelm Marx, Centre Party leader and candidate of the 'Weimar' parties.

On the face of things, Hindenburg's accession to the Presidency was an ominous development from the point of view of supporters of the Republic. A monarchist and honorary chairman of the *Stahlhelm*, he had been backed by 14 million Germans and was now in a position to undermine Weimar from within. In fact Hindenburg, at least until 1930, conducted himself in public in a generally restrained and non-partisan way. There were occasions, though, on which he made plain his anti-Weimar sympathies. In 1926 he openly opposed a KPD-SPD proposal to nationalise property belonging to Germany's former royal families. Later in the same year, and even more controversially, he issued a decree stipulating that Germany's embassies abroad should fly a black-red-white flag – the colours of the pre-1918 Empire – alongside the black-red-gold colours of the Weimar Republic. Whether the Republic was safe in Hindenburg's hands was therefore open to doubt .

Political violence

Political violence in the later 1920s assumed new forms. Nothing took place resembling the Spartacist rising or the Kapp Putsch, but there were calculated attempts to challenge the authorities by lawless and violent means. Here it was the Nazis who took the lead. On his release from prison in December 1924, Hitler committed the NSDAP to the so-called policy of 'legality'. It entailed contesting elections with the object of building a power base in the Reichstag while simultaneously using the SA to destabilise the Republic by street violence. Between 1924 and 1929, 24 Nazis were killed in street fighting with the KPD and hundreds were injured. Berlin was the scene of many of the worst clashes, thanks in part to the activities of Josef Goebbels, appointed Gauleiter (area leader) of Berlin by Hitler in 1926 with a brief to build up Nazi support in the capital. Nazi aggressiveness was matched by that of the KPD and its paramilitary force, the 120,000 strong *Rote Frontkämpferbund* (Red Fighting League), founded in 1924. The *Rote Frontkämpferbund* did battle with the authorities, with the SA and with the SPD's paramilitary organisation, the *Reichsbanner*. One especially brutal clash between the KPD and the authorities in Berlin in May 1929 left 30 dead and 200 injured. A political system in which there was such ready and widespread resort to the club, knuckle-duster, broken bottle and revolver clearly cannot be said to be a healthy one. Paramilitary violence was to intensify in the early 1930s.

Figure 6
Cartoon from the satirical magazine *Simplicissimus*, 1924. The helpless carthorse is the Republic itself (the head is President Ebert) and its armed and uniformed paramilitary tormentors are the Nazis (swastika) and Communists (star).

Whether or not the years between 1924 and 1929 can reasonably be described as 'golden' depends in the end on the perspective from which they are viewed. If they are compared with what preceded them within Germany (the turmoil of 1919–23) and with what followed them (depression and Nazi dictatorship) then they were indeed 'golden'. If, alternatively, Germany in these years is compared to other democratic states, 'golden years' scarcely seems appropriate. In comparison with 1920s Britain, for example, Weimar Germany in its middle years was a tense, disturbed and seriously divided society. Britain had more than its share of economic difficulties in the 1920s and there were fierce conflicts between employers and labour too. Unlike Germany, however, Britain did not have large numbers of the population fundamentally opposed to the arrangements under which the country was governed. Nor did politics in Britain have the paramilitary dimension they did in Germany.

Studying 'The "golden years" of Weimar'

1 This chapter is organised thematically rather than chronologically. A time chart showing key events in the years 1923–29 might therefore be of use. Include in the chart Stresemann's resignation as Chancellor; the Dawes plan; the Locarno Pact; Germany's entry into the League of Nations; Hindenburg's election as President; the 'flag controversy' started by Hindenburg; the passage of the Labour Exchanges and Unemployment Insurance Act; the Ruhr steel lock-out; Reichstag elections; the formation of the *Rote Frontkämpferbund*.

2 You will need to understand the aims and achievements of Stresemann's diplomacy and the reasons why it was controversial within Germany.

a) List the specific aims of Stresemann's foreign policy and assess the extent to which each was achieved

b) In what ways did Britain and France revise the 1919–21 treaty arrangements with Germany in the years 1924–29?

c) 'The enslavement of Germany': why did the extreme right believe this to be the outcome of Stresemann's foreign policy?

3 a) The question arises of who deserves most credit for the 'relative stabilisation' of Weimar Germany in the years 1924–29. Assess the claims of each of the following, trying to place them in rank order and giving reasons for your choice: Gustav Stresemann; American investors; Weimar artists and writers; President Hindenburg; the trades unions; employers; Britain and France.

b) 'The survival of the Weimar Republic in 1923 and its stability in the years 1923–29 owes everything to Stresemann.' How far would you accept this opinion?

4 Draw up a balance sheet for the period 1924–29 showing:

a) reasons for optimism, and

b) reasons for pessimism about the Weimar Republic's survival prospects.

5 Last years, 1930–33

The collapse of democratic government, the struggle to create a more authoritarian system, and the rise of Hitler and the Nazis

---

Key points

◆ Democratic government as envisaged by the Weimar constitution broke down in 1930
◆ How have historians explained the post-1930 Nazi electoral breakthrough?
◆ Between 1930 and 1933 Schleicher tried to replace Weimar democracy with an authoritarian political system
◆ In the end Hitler out-manoeuvred Schleicher and his other right-wing rivals

---

The last phase of the Weimar Republic's history was ushered in by economic depression. The post-1929 slump was, of course, a world-wide affair, but Germany was especially severely affected. The main reason for this was the German economy's excessive dependence on foreign loans and credits. In 1929 American investors, devastated by the Wall Street Crash, scrambled to get their money out of Germany, leaving many German businesses with more or less insoluble cash-flow problems. In addition, German exporters were badly hit by the post-1929 contraction of world trade. The principal consequence of the slump, in Germany as elsewhere, was unemployment. Between 1929 and 1932 the number out of work rose sharply, peaking at nearly 6 million – nearly 30% of the workforce. Nor did those in work escape the effects of the slump: they were hit by short-time working and wage cuts.

Why did parliamentary government break down in 1930?

At the core of the Weimar political system was the principle of parliamentary government. Parliamentary government means rule by a government drawn from, and accountable to, parliament. In March 1930 parliamentary government in Germany broke down irretrievably.

Between 1928 and 1930 Germany was governed by a 'grand coalition' consisting of the middle-class parties (the DVP, Centre and DDP) and the SPD. When unemployment began to soar, the middle-class parties, conservative in economic outlook, argued for reductions in public spending and cuts in unemployment benefit. To the SPD, with its supporters badly hit by unemployment, these proposals were entirely unacceptable. With his government in hopeless disarray, the Chancellor, Hermann Müller of the SPD, was forced to resign. At this point parliamentary government became impossible. The middle-class parties and the SPD were unable to agree among themselves; neither the middle-class parties nor the SPD had enough support within the Reichstag to govern on their own; and there was, needless to say, no possibility of the 'anti-Weimar' parties (KPD, DNVP and Nazis) helping to salvage things by entering government. In these circumstances the only option was 'presidential' government on the basis of Article 48 of the constitution.

The outcome of the Reichstag elections of 1930 and 1932 put paid to any chance of a return to parliamentary government. In 1930 the four 'Weimar' parties (the SPD, DDP, Centre Party and DVP) won only 48% of the vote between them and would therefore have been unable to form a viable government even if they had been able to overcome their differences. In 1932 their combined share of the vote slipped to 40% (July) and then to 38% (November). Meanwhile the share of the vote won by the 'anti-Weimar' parties rose sharply. In 1928 the KPD, DNVP and Nazis had won only 27% of the vote between them. This figure rose to 38% in 1930 and to 57% in July 1932. It was the Nazis who made the most spectacular gains.

Who voted Nazi?

The surge in electoral support for the Nazis which took place between 1928 and 1932 was extraordinary. In the 1928 Reichstag elections, only 810,127 Germans voted for the NSDAP: in July 1932 13,765,781 did so. The NSDAP share of the vote leapt from 2.6% in 1928 to 37.4% in July 1932. Not surprisingly, given the consequences of the Nazi breakthrough, the question of where these votes came from is one which has been intensively researched by historians.

Until the 1980s historians believed that the Nazi electoral breakthrough was based very largely on the votes of the urban and rural middle classes – especially the Protestant middle classes. In the early 1930s, it was suggested, the middle classes were terrified that Germany would succumb to what was called 'the Russian solution' – Communist dictatorship – and turned to the Nazis because they appeared more capable than any other political party or movement of halting Communism in its tracks. The Nazis' reputation for brutality, which had previously alienated the 'respectable' middle classes, now became a positive asset. A corollary of the view that the Nazis' electoral support was middle class in origin was that the working classes were largely impervious to their appeal.

There is a mass of evidence which can be offered in support of this 'middle class' interpretation of the Nazis' electoral success. Two points in particular should be noted.

◆ During the period in which the Nazis were gaining electoral ground the middle-class parties (the DVP, DDP and DNVP) lost votes but support for the SPD and Centre Party remained comparatively stable. This suggests that middle-class voters were changing their allegiance but working-class and Catholic voters were not.

◆ In the early 1930s the Nazis polled most strongly in Protestant smaller towns and rural districts of the north German plain, less strongly in the major cities and least strongly of all in the Catholic areas in the west and

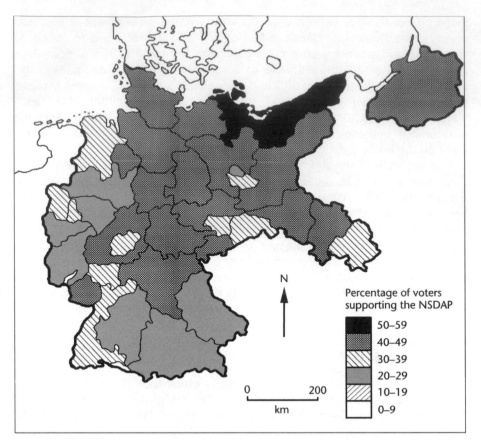

Figure 7
The electoral geography of
Nazism in the early 1930s.
(NB This map relates to
the second round of the
1932 presidential election:
a similar pattern is evident
in the Reichstag elections
of 1930, 1932 and 1933.)

Percentage of voters
supporting the NSDAP

50–59
40–49
30–39
20–29
10–19
0–9

south of the country (see Figure 7). In the major cities the Nazi vote was lower in the working-class districts than it was in the middle-class suburbs. This pattern is consistent with the 'middle class' interpretation.

Recent research has not overturned the 'middle class' interpretation of the Nazis' electoral breakthrough but it has modified it in a number of respects.

◆ In the 1930 election 1.7 million young voters went to the polls for the first time. In 1930, moreover, turnout was 6% higher than it had been in 1928, meaning that more than 2 million people voted in the 1930 election who had not voted in 1928. In all, therefore, over 4 million of those who voted in the Nazis' breakthrough election were new voters.

◆ The Nazis aimed to turn themselves into a 'people's party' which cut across class barriers and succeeded in doing so to a greater extent than was once thought. They became what the historian Hans Mommsen calls "a catch-all party of protest" by targeting specific social and occupational groups and successfully exploiting their particular grievances. Prominent among the groups courted by the Nazis were Germany's hard-pressed farmers. Operating through Walther Darré's Agricultural Affairs Bureau, the Nazis lured farmers with promises of tax cuts and increased tariffs on imported food. Young people were another of the Nazis' targets. They sought, with considerable success, to attract the young with a style of politics more dynamic and colourful than anything on offer from the older-established parties and by projecting themselves as the party of youth. Another successful ploy of the Nazis was to stigmatise other political parties as tools of special interest groups and to suggest that the Nazis alone had the capacity to build a genuine *Volksgemeinschaft* ('national community').

◆ There were more working-class Nazi voters than was previously thought. Conan Fischer estimates that 40% of all Nazi voters belonged to the working classes. The workers who voted Nazi, though, were more likely to be self-employed craftsmen or non-unionised employees of small firms than members of SPD-linked trades unions. The SPD and its unions offered their members not just political and industrial representation but a whole way of life, including newspapers, libraries, evening classes and sports teams. Once part of this world people tended not break away from it.

'Presidential' government

'Presidential' government did not involve Hindenburg personally taking up the reins of government. This was out of the question. The President was 83-years-old in 1930 and was not in full possession of his faculties. In the early 1930s, according to the American journalist John Gunther, a story went the rounds in Berlin that Hindenburg, watching a paramilitary march-past, turned to his son and said "I had no idea we had taken so many Russians prisoner".

Hindenburg's role in the era of 'presidential' government (1930–33) consisted of appointing and dismissing Chancellors and putting his name to decrees as and when necessary. In exercising these powers he was strongly influenced by the group of advisers and courtiers which surrounded him. They included his son Oscar, an army officer in his 50s, and his state secretary, Otto Meissner. Hindenburg's most influential adviser, though, was Major-General Kurt von Schleicher, a senior official in the Defence Ministry and at this time political mouthpiece of the *Reichswehr*.

Shrewd, ambitious and manipulative, Schleicher saw the collapse of parliamentary government as an opportunity to reconstruct the German political system on a non-democratic basis. It was an opportunity he and others in Hindenburg's entourage were eager to take. What they had in mind was a kind of bloodless conservative revolution. Weimar democracy, it can be argued, ended when 'presidential' government began: what remained was the question of which particular form of right-wing authoritarianism would establish itself in its place.

Brüning's Chancellorship, 1930–32

Between March 1930 and May 1932 Germany's Chancellor was the able but colourless and inflexible Heinrich Brüning, a right-wing member of the Centre Party. Essentially Brüning was Schleicher's nominee. The qualities which led Schleicher to recommend him to Hindenburg in 1930 were his expertise in finance, his authoritarian political leanings and, not least, his military record. Brüning had been a front-line officer in the war and had been decorated for bravery. Schleicher also hoped, correctly as it turned out, that the 'Weimar' parties in the Reichstag would at least tolerate Brüning's rule. After the Nazi electoral breakthrough in September 1930 the moderates had little choice: the alternative to Brüning seemed likely to be Hitler.

As Chancellor, Brüning aimed to boost the competitiveness of Germany's export industries by cutting costs at home and to ensure the stability of the mark by keeping public spending under tight control. He therefore reduced

	Communists	Nazis	Total
1930	44	17	61
1931	52	42	94
1932	75	84	159

Figure 8
Political violence 1930–32: number of Communists and Nazis killed.

unemployment benefits, imposed wage cuts on public employees and increased both direct and indirect taxes. This programme was deflationary in its effects – that is, it reduced the level of activity in the German economy – and it did nothing to halt the rise in unemployment. Brüning's austerity policy earned him the nickname of 'the hunger Chancellor'

Brüning's Chancellorship came to an end in 1932 because he lost the confidence of his two patrons, Schleicher and Hindenburg. Schleicher was frustrated by Brüning's inability to bring down the jobless total and he was also alarmed by the deteriorating public order situation. Clashes between Communists and Nazis had increased sharply in scale and ferocity since 1930 (see Figure 8). Schleicher reached the conclusion that a more right-wing Chancellor was needed, one who could do business with Hitler.

Brüning offended Hindenburg in two ways. First, in 1932 Brüning failed to persuade the Nazis and the DNVP to allow an extension of Hindenburg's term as President. At 85 Hindenburg was forced to fight an election. Much to his dismay, he failed to win an overall majority on the first ballot and in the second round defeated his main rival, Hitler, by the comparatively unimpressive margin of 19 million votes to 13 million.

Brüning's second offence was to antagonise the Prussian nobility, the Junkers, owners of estates in the depressed eastern part of Germany. By 1932 many Junkers were in acute financial difficulties, despite the fact that since 1928 they had received large subsidies from public funds via the 'Aid to the East' (*Osthilfe*) programme. Brüning's response to this situation was to draw up plans to break up the most hopelessly bankrupt Junker estates and turn them into peasant smallholdings. Outraged Junkers complained to Hindenburg, a Junker himself, that Brüning was no more than an 'agrarian Bolshevik'. It sealed his political fate.

Von Papen as Chancellor, June–December 1932

Brüning's successor as Chancellor was Franz von Papen, a right-wing Catholic aristocrat who before 1932 was virtually a political unknown. Like Brüning, von Papen was Schleicher's nominee.

There was no expectation on Schleicher's part that von Papen's government would, like Brüning's, be 'tolerated' by the 'Weimar' parties. Von Papen's appointment was the result of a rightwards shift in his political thinking. In 1932 Schleicher abandoned the idea of winning acceptance for 'presidential' government among political moderates and became intent on establishing a more overtly authoritarian system which brought together the traditional élites (the army, industrialists and Junkers, for example) and the Nazis. Schleicher believed the Nazis could be 'tamed' within such a system. Von Papen was part of Schleicher's plans mainly because he was well connected within the traditional élites. Schleicher also saw 'little Franz' as a political lightweight who could be relied upon to do as he was told.

In mid-1932 Schleicher and von Papen set out to woo the Nazis in a number of ways.

◆ Extreme right-wing ministers, several belonging to the DNVP, were appointed to serve under von Papen. Schleicher himself became defence minister. The government became known as 'the cabinet of barons'.

◆ A ban imposed on the SA in April 1932 was lifted in June.

◆ The state government of Prussia, hated by Nazis and other right-wingers because key departments in it were headed by SPD ministers, was deposed by presidential decree in July 1932. The federal government took over responsibility for Prussia's affairs, von Papen himself becoming Minister-President of Prussia. The seizure of power in Prussia meant that Germany ceased to be a federal state of the kind envisaged in the 1919 constitution, with power shared between the state (*Land*) and federal governments.

◆ Reichstag elections were called for July, giving the Nazis an opportunity to strengthen their electoral base. In these elections the Nazis made sweeping gains.

Schleicher's plans went awry after the elections of July 1932. Hitler, contrary to Schleicher's expectations, refused to serve under von Papen and demanded the Chancellorship for himself. Hitler also insisted that his appointment as Chancellor be accompanied by the passage of an Enabling Bill that would amend the constitution and free him from any dependence on the President. When he put these demands directly to Hindenburg at a meeting in August, he was icily snubbed. Hitler retaliated by ordering his followers in the Reichstag to support a vote of no confidence in von Papen as Chancellor. The passing of this vote in September necessitated new Reichstag elections which were scheduled for November.

At this point there was another development unwelcome from Schleicher's view: von Papen asserted his political independence. In the course of 1932 'little Franz' had wormed his way into Hindenburg's affections. He now came forward with plans to make himself Germany's dictator. They involved the more or less permanent suspension of the Reichstag and the use of the army to suppress opposition from any quarter. Schleicher responded by pressurising Hindenburg into dismissing von Papen, telling him that the *Reichswehr* was opposed to von Papen's plans. He took over as Chancellor himself.

Schleicher's Chancellorship, December 1932–January 1933

Schleicher's position as Chancellor was precarious from the outset, mainly because he did not have the full confidence of the President. Hindenburg resented the loss of his beloved von Papen and blamed it on Schleicher. In addition von Papen was thirsting for revenge and in order to get it was prepared to form a political alliance with Hitler. Schleicher pinned his hopes for survival on a far-fetched scheme which involved rallying the trades unions and the anti-capitalist or 'socialistic' wing of the NSDAP led by Gregor Strasser behind a programme of work creation. The scheme came to nothing. The unions distrusted Schleicher and the hoped-for split within the NSDAP did not take place. Schleicher resigned as Chancellor on 28 January.

Schleicher's resignation ended a three-year period during which he had been the most influential figure in German politics. His aim had been to put in place an authoritarian political system in which Germany's traditional élites, above all the army, had a controlling interest. There were a number of reasons for his failure, among them Hindenburg's unreliability, von Papen's disloyalty and the growing impatience of the *Reichswehr* with his intrigues. Probably the most important reason for Schleicher's failure, though, was that Hitler was too shrewd and too powerful to be 'tamed'.

The Nazi seizure of power

After Schleicher's resignation, Hitler was appointed Chancellor with von Papen as his Vice-Chancellor. This arrangement was brokered by von Papen. Only von Papen could have overcome Hindenburg's aversion to Hitler. He did so by assuring Hindenburg that he could succeed in 'taming' Hitler where others had failed.

When Hitler took office he was a 'presidential' Chancellor of the kind that Brüning, von Papen and Schleicher had been before him. Moreover, only three of his 12-strong cabinet were Nazis. In other words, Hitler in January 1933 had only limited power when what he wanted was absolute power. The only way absolute power could be achieved lawfully was by amending or abolishing the Weimar constitution. What this involved in practice was an Enabling Act – an Act which, because it was a constitutional amendment, could only become law if it was supported by a two-thirds majority in the Reichstag. If, therefore, the Nazis were to secure the passage of an Enabling Act, they first had to strengthen their position in the Reichstag. This meant a further round of Reichstag elections.

The election of March 1933 in Germany was neither fair nor genuinely free. The Nazis were intent on victory at any cost. Early in the election campaign SA men were enrolled as auxiliary policemen and proceeded to attack and intimidate the NSDAP's opponents. In Prussia, where Göring, Hitler's chief lieutenant, had become Minister of the Interior, Communist, SPD and Centre Party newspapers were suppressed. Then, on the eve of the poll, came the burning-down of the Reichstag building, allegedly by Marinus van der Lubbe, a Dutch vagrant with Communist connections, but in all probability by the SA or the SS. The Reichstag fire allowed the Nazis to claim that a Communist uprising was imminent. A state of emergency was declared. A presidential order ('Decree for the Protection of the People and the State') was issued suspending a number of the individual rights guaranteed by the 1919 constitution. In the next few days the KPD was effectively destroyed as an organised political force.

In the event the Nazis failed to win their overall majority (see reference section, Table 2). This, however, did not prevent the passage of the Enabling Act. The 81-strong KPD delegation was excluded from the Reichstag (most of them were under arrest) and the 52 DNVP deputies supported the Nazis. The Centre Party also voted for the Enabling Act, misguidedly believing that Hitler might offer favours in return. 26 SPD deputies were absent. The Enabling Act was passed on 23 March by 444–94. With its passage the Weimar Republic formally came to an end.

The one remaining link with Weimar after March 1933 was Hindenburg, who was allowed to retain the title of President. When Hindenburg died in 1934 Hitler abolished the Presidency and gave himself the title of 'Führer and Reich Chancellor'.

Hitler's political skill

Because the NSDAP did not win an overall majority in any of the elections of the early 1930s, Hitler was never in a position to demand political power as a matter of absolute democratic right. He was therefore obliged to manoeuvre for position. In the process he showed himself to be an unscrupulous but skilled and resourceful political operator.

◆ His energy and skill as an orator and propagandist sustained the Nazis through three punishing national election campaigns in 1932.

◆ He resisted the attempts of a number of other right-wing leaders to 'tame' the Nazi movement for their own ends – first Hugenberg, whose DNVP in 1931–32 formed a short-lived political alliance with the Nazis known as the 'Harzburg Front', then Schleicher and von Papen.

◆ He displayed a great deal of political nerve and self-belief. Examples are his challenge to Hindenburg, idol of the nationalist right, in the presidential election of 1932; his refusal to take the Chancellorship in 1932–33 except on his own terms; and his coolness in late 1932 in the face of Schleicher's attempts to split the NSDAP.

Studying 'The last years, 1930–33'

1   As with other chapters, events have not been described here in strict chronological order, and a time chart is therefore a useful starting point for independent study. Include the following in your time chart: the fall of Müller's 'grand coalition'; the appointment, and fall, as Chancellor of Brüning, von Papen and Schleicher; the Reichstag elections of 1930, 1932 (two) and 1933; the presidential election of 1932; von Papen's seizure of power in Prussia; Hindenburg's snubbing of Hitler in 1932; Hitler's appointment as Chancellor; the Reichstag fire; passage of the Enabling Act.

2   There are a number of terms you will need to understand. Write a sentence explaining the meaning of each of the following: parliamentary government; presidential government; conservative revolution; 'toleration' (as used to describe the attitude of 'Weimar' parties to Brüning's government); deflation.

3   Democracy in Germany had already been seriously eroded long before Hitler passed the Enabling Act. Write a paragraph explaining why each of the following was an important stage in the erosion of democracy in Germany: Brüning's appointment as Chancellor; von Papen's appointment as Chancellor; von Papen's seizure of power in Prussia, 1932; the 'Decree for the Protection of the People and the State', 1933.

4   What were the causes of the fall as Chancellor of (a) Brüning (b) von Papen, and (c) Schleicher?

5   Why did Schleicher's plans for a 'conservative revolution' fail?

6   How true is it to say that Hitler acquired power by entirely legal means? In your answer consider the legality, or otherwise, of the SA's campaign of violence, 1930–33; the way in which Hitler became Chancellor in January 1933; the use of the SA as auxiliary policemen in the 1933 election campaign; the 'Decree for the Protection of the People and the State'; the manner in which the Enabling Act was passed.

6 Historical interpretations

How have historians explained the failure of the Weimar Republic?

Key points

- Extreme right-wing and extreme left-wing interpretations of Weimar's failure are now generally disregarded
- There is general agreement among historians over the causes of failure, but disagreement over how much weight should be attached to each cause
- Was the failure of the Republic inevitable?

Propaganda and history

The first explanation of the Weimar Republic's downfall was that of the Nazis. This was taught in German schools during the era of the Third Reich. According to the Nazis, Germans rejected the Republic because they could not stomach betrayal and corruption. After 1918, it was argued, Germany was betrayed by the 'November criminals' and corrupted by Jewish racketeers. In this version of events Hitler was depicted as a national hero who had awakened the German people to the Republic's evils.

The Nazi account of the Weimar Republic's history was, of course, a tissue of lies and distortions. It was propaganda, not history, and since the collapse of the Third Reich it has had no serious defenders. Historians do not even accept that Hitler and the Nazis were a major cause of the Republic's collapse. "The growth of the Nazi movement . . . was not the reason for the deepening crisis of Weimar parliamentarism, but rather its consequence. The democratic system was virtually destroyed before Hitler could claim to replace it by an alleged fundamentally new political order. . . . It is utterly misleading to claim that the National Socialist attack on the Republic was the main reason for its downfall" (Hans Mommsen, 1988).

Scholarly, research-based study of the Weimar era began only after 1945. It is now "one of the best-researched periods of German history" (Eberhard Kolb, 1988). P. D. Stachura's *The Weimar Era and Hitler, 1918–1933*, a bibliography published in Britain in 1977, listed more than 3,000 titles. Kolb's 1988 survey of historical writing about the Weimar Republic, confined in its author's words to 'essential aspects' only, makes reference to over 700 works.

The nature of the debate among historians

The history of the Weimar Republic has been written by British and American as well as by German historians. In the early post-war years nationality was a factor which shaped the kinds of interpretation historians offered of the Republic's collapse. Some British and American historians maintained that Weimar failed because too many Germans lacked democratic instincts while patriotic German historians defended their country by pointing to the role of chance in the Republic's downfall or by suggesting that ultra-nationalism was in the 1920s and 1930s a force at work not just in Germany but across the whole of Western Europe. Examples of anti-German writing from this period by British and American historians are *The Course of German History* (1945) by A. J. P. Taylor and *The Rise and Fall of the Third Reich* (1960) by the American journalist-come-historian William Shirer. German defences against this kind of attack include *Die Deutsche Katastrophe* (1946) by Friedrich Meinecke and *Europe und die deutsche Frage* (1948) by Gerhard Ritter.

Not surprisingly, historians born since 1945 have been able to write about inter-war Germany in a more detached and objective way than writers like Shirer or Meinecke who lived through the Nazi era. There are certainly no signs of anti-German prejudice in recent British and American work on the Weimar Republic. Nationality is no longer a significant influence on the kinds of interpretation historians offer of the Republic's downfall.

Historians often disagree in their interpretation of events because they write from differing political or ideological standpoints. A socialist historian, for example, is likely to be more critical than a conservative historian of the Poor Law in 19th-century Britain, and a Marxist historian who believes that revolutions are caused by class conflict is unlikely to take the same view of events in France in 1789 as a non-Marxist historian who does not start from this assumption. Disagreements of this kind are not absent from historical writing about the Weimar Republic.

Between 1949 and 1990 there were two Germanies. East German historians who published studies of Weimar history in these years wrote from a Communist perspective. In East German accounts of the Weimar Republic, the Spartacists were heroes and the Majority Socialists and German capitalists were villains, the former because they made an alliance with conservative forces in 1918–19 to defeat Communism and the latter because they aided Hitler financially. West German historians in general took a dim view of biased writing of this kind, though Eberhard Kolb points out that the work of East German historians is not valueless because it made use of sources which were not available to Western scholars while Germany was divided. The reunification of Germany in 1990 effectively brought to an end historical writing about the Weimar Republic from a Communist perspective. Nowadays historians of Weimar Germany are biased neither to the extreme left or the extreme right.

The history of the Weimar Republic is not, then, a battleground on which historians of different nationalities and radically divergent political views line up against each other. Among recent historians there is in fact as much agreement as there is disagreement on the reasons for the Republic's failure. Where differences do occur, it is the susceptibility of the available evidence to more than one interpretation rather than the nationality or political outlook of the historians concerned that is responsible.

Four points can be made about the current state of debate on the question of the Weimar Republic's failure.

◆ Few, if any, historians now accept monocausal explanations of the Republic's failure which emphasise one cause – proportional representation, for instance – at the expense of all others. There were many reasons for the Republic's failure and not just one: a multi-causal explanation is therefore required.

◆ Historians are to a large extent agreed on what the principal causes of the Republic's failure were.

◆ There is, however, a good deal of disagreement among historians about the relative importance of these causes.

◆ Some historians believe that the Republic's failure was more or less inevitable: others do not.

The causes of the Weimar Republic's failure

The main factors which feature in discussions of the Weimar Republic's failure are set out below.

◆ The Republic was faced with deep-rooted economic difficulties. Territorial losses, war debts and reparations made Germany a significantly poorer country after 1918 than it had been before 1914, but in the 1920s the German people expected a return to pre-war levels of prosperity. When these expectations were not met disillusionment became widespread. According to the left-wing Weimar satirist Kurt Tucholsky, it became an article of faith among middle-class Germans in the 1920s that 'Under the Kaiser everything was better'.

◆ The Weimar Republic was gravely damaged by outside forces and developments over which Weimar politicians had more or less no control: examples include the Versailles Treaty, the French occupation of the Ruhr and the post-1929 depression, each of which had massive implications for the Republic's stability.

◆ Weimar Germany's political culture – that is, the values, beliefs and instincts which shaped political behaviour – was heavily influenced by the authoritarian political culture of Wilhelmine Germany. It appears likely, for example, that in the Weimar era "the vast majority of the middle class was still under the sway of authoritarian ideas" (Karl Dietrich Bracher, *The German Dictatorship*, 1969). It is also the case that the three original pro-Weimar parties (the SDP, the Centre Party and the DDP) between them won an absolute majority of votes cast only in the election of 1919: thereafter they were in a minority. "The most pervasive cause of Weimar's failure", writes E. J. Feuchtwanger (*From Weimar to Hitler*, 1995) "was that too many Germans did not regard it as a legitimate regime."

◆ The élites of Wilhelmine Germany – the army, industrialists, university professors and the judiciary, for example – retained much of their power after 1918 and used it to destabilise the Republic.

◆ The Weimar Republic lacked inspirational political leadership. "While Walter Rathenau and Gustav Stresemann steered Germany towards a reasonable course in foreign affairs . . . no dynamic leaders on the national level commanded the broad popular appeal needed to rally support for the Republic. A magnetic Republican leader could have been a significant force for the creation of more Republicans." (Paul Bookbinder, *Weimar Germany: The Republic of the Reasonable*, 1996).

◆ Germany's multi-party system – a reflection of underlying divisions and tensions within German society – meant that short-lived and relatively weak governments were almost inevitable. The prevalence of such governments eroded confidence in the political system and gave rise to cynicism about it.

◆ There were specific weaknesses within the Weimar constitution which gave scope to its enemies. In particular, Article 48 of the constitution equipped the President with powers which could in anti-Weimar hands, such as those of Hindenburg, be used to undermine the Republic. Article 48 also meant that the parties in the Reichstag were not under the same kind of pressure as political parties were in a fully parliamentary system like Britain's to find solutions in times of crisis, even if these meant disagreeable compromises. Weimar parties were able to pass the buck to the President. The system of proportional representation used in elections could be said to be a further weakness of the constitution in that it contributed to political instability, but on this point it should be noted that the German Federal Republic, which also operates a system of proportional representation, has since 1949 been a model of political stability. It is true, however, that proportional representation made it easy for extremist parties to win seats in the Reichstag, thus giving them political credibility when they lacked widespread popular support.

It is difficult to generalise about the differing weightings historians attach to these causes. Weimar's economic problems and the authoritarian political culture it inherited are often given precedence over other causes of failure, but there are historians who insist that the search for reasons for Weimar's collapse must begin with international relations and the burdens placed on Germany by the Allies. It is also frequently pointed out that Weimar was not brought down by this or that cause but rather by the combined weight of the problems it faced. "In considering the collapse of the Weimar Republic" writes Knut Borchardt, "we should ask whether the problem did not lie in the accumulation of causal factors, each of which may not on its own have proved decisive, but which when put together proved disruptive" (*Perspectives on Modern German Economic History and Policy*, 1991).

Was the failure of the Weimar Republic inevitable?

Historians who believe that Weimar's failure was more or less inevitable can be termed 'pessimists' and those do not can be described as 'optimists'.

Among historians based in Britain, Richard Bessel is a leading exponent of the 'pessimistic' view. Weimar, says Bessel, quoting the German historian Gerald Feldman, was "a gamble which stood virtually no chance of success". Bessel emphasises the seriousness of the economic problems facing Weimar governments, which left them with little room for manoeuvre. He points as well to the German people's expectations of a return to prosperity. In these circumstances, he maintains, Weimar politicians were unable to take the tough measures needed to improve the economy in the longer term. The result was that Weimar governments found it impossible to create a wide base of popular support for the Republic.

Bessel's views are influenced by those of the German economic historian Knut Borchardt. Borchardt maintains that even in the 'golden years' of 1924–29, the Weimar economy was abnormal and even sick. Rates of economic growth, he suggests, were not sufficiently high to allow all politically important groups to become better off. In the slowly-growing Weimar economy, gains for some sections of the community necessarily meant losses for others. In general, according to Borchardt, the gainers in the later 1920s were trades unions and employers and the middle classes were the losers. As a result, the employers and middle classes, the latter still reeling from the impact of hyper-inflation, came to favour a more authoritarian form of government as a way of regaining their strength. Nor, says Borchardt, would things have been better if the unions had agreed to wage curbs. In this event the unions would have lost ground to 'radical forces' – the Communists – and the Republic would have been under threat from the extreme left rather than the extreme right. In Borchardt's model, everyone was trapped.

Prominent 'optimists' among British historians are John Hiden and E. J. Feuchtwanger. The 'optimists' are impressed by the Weimar Republic's resilience. They point to the way in which it survived the severe crises of its early years. What defeated it in the end, say the 'optimists', was the enormity of the problems associated with the post-1929 depression. "There was until the final years of the republic little reason to suppose that the diverse and ill-assorted 'national opposition' could be formed into a battering ram to destroy the republic. It needed the extreme pressure of the great depression to marshal these diverse forces and ideas behind national socialism and Hitler" (E. J. Feuchtwanger, *From Weimar to Hitler*, 1995).

Further reading

There is a full survey of historical writing about the Weimar Republic in Eberhard Kolb, *The Weimar Republic* (London, 1988) and a briefer treatment by P. D. Stachura in 'Weimar, National Socialism and Historians' in P. D. Stachura (ed.), *The Nazi Machtergreifung* (London, 1983). Richard Bessel's 'pessimistic' view is set out in 'Why did the Weimar Republic collapse?', a contribution to I. Kershaw (ed.) *Weimar: Why Did German Democracy Fail?* (London, 1990). The 'optimistic' view developed at length by E. J. Feuchtwanger in *From Weimar to Hitler: Germany 1918–33* (2nd edn, London, 1995) is summarised in 'Weimar's Thin Thread for Survival Snapped by Political Errors' in *New Perspectives for Modern History Students* (vol.1, no. 1, September 1995). The views of leading German historians of the Weimar Republic like Hans Mommsen and Eberhard Jäckel can be found in accessible form in Michael Laffan (ed.), *The Burden of German History* 1919–45 (London, 1988).

Two recent additions to the Manchester University Press's 'New Frontiers in History' series offer detailed and valuable, though not undemanding, studies of aspects of Weimar history: Conan Fischer, *The Rise of the Nazis* (1995) and Paul Bookbinder, *Weimar Germany: The Republic of the Reasonable* (1996). A. Kaes, M. Jay and E. Dimendberg, *The Weimar Republic Sourcebook* (University of California Press) is a collection of primary source material in translation, much of it focusing on Weimar culture. A. J. Nicholls, *Weimar and the Rise of Hitler* (3rd edn, London, 1991) is the standard introduction to the Republic's political history.

Table 1: Political parties in the Weimar Republic

PARTY	GERMAN NAME	PROMINENT FIGURES	ASSOCIATED PARAMILITARY FORCE	POLITICAL STANCE	ELECTORAL SUPPORT
Nazis (NSDAP)	National Sozialistische Deutsche Arbeiterpartei	Adolf Hitler (1889–1945) Hermann Göring (1893–1946)	Sturmabteilung (SA)	◆ Anti-Weimar ◆ Anti-monarchist ◆ Extreme right-wing	Predominantly middle class, but to some degree a 'catch-all party of protest'
Nationalists (DNVP)	Deutschnationale Volkspartei (DNVP)	Karl Helfferich (1872–1924) Count von Westarp (1864–1945) Alfred Hugenberg (1865–1951)	Stahlhelm	◆ Anti-Weimar ◆ Monarchist ◆ Extreme right-wing	Junkers Industrialists Farmers Some middle class
People's Party (DVP)	Deutsche Volkspartei (DVP)	Gustav Stresemann (1878–1929)		◆ Initially anti-Weimar, then supportive under Stresemann ◆ Right-wing liberal	Upper middle classes Business community
Centre Party	Zentrum	Matthias Erzberger (1875–1921) Josef Wirth (1879–1956) Heinrich Brüning (1885–1970)		◆ Pro-Weimar Catholic. ◆ Flexible and internally divided on non-religious issues	Upper and middle class Catholics with strong working-class wing in the Rhineland
Democratic Party (DDP)	Deutsche Demokratische Partei (DDP)	Hugo Preuss (1860–1925) Walter Rathenau (1867–1922)		◆ Pro-Weimar ◆ Left-wing liberal	Intellectuals Some professional classes Germany's Jewish community
Social Democrats (SDP)	Sozialdemokratische Partei Deutschlands (SDP)	Friedrich Ebert (1871–1925) Philip Scheidemann (1865–1939) Gustav Noske (1868–1946) Hermann Müller (1876–1931)	Reichsbanner	◆ Pro-Weimar. ◆ Moderate 'reformist' socialist	Industrial working class Some lower middle class
Communists (KPD)	Kommunistische Partei Deutschlands (KPD)	Karl Liebknecht (1871–1919) Rosa Luxemburg (1870–1919) Ernst Thälmann (1886–1944)	Rote Frontkämpfbund (Red Fighting League)	◆ Anti-Weimar ◆ Revolutionary socialist	Industrial working class

Table 2: Reichstag elections, 1919–33 (% of votes cast for each party)

PARTY	1919	1920	1924 (May)	1924 (Dec.)	1928	1930	1932 (July)	1932 (Nov.)	1933
KPD	–	2	12	9	11	13	14	17	12
USPD	8	17	1	–	–	-	–	–	–
SDP	38	21	21	26	30	24	22	20	19
DDP	19	8	6	6	5	4	1	1	1
Centre Party	20	18	17	18	15	15	16	15	14
DVP	4	14	9	10	9	5	1	2	1
DNVP	10	15	19	21	14	7	6	9	8
NSDAP (Nazis)	–	–	7	3	2	18	37	33	44
Others	1	5	8	7	14	14	3	3	1

NOTES
*The result shown for 1919 that of the Constituent Assembly election and is therefore not, strictly speaking, the result of a Reichstag election
**The USPD (Independent Socialist Party) more or less disintegrated in 1920–22: its left wing joined the KPD and its (bigger) right wing rejoined the SPD

Table 3: Weimar governments, 1919–30 (■ = membership of a government)

Dates	Chancellor (party in brackets)	Nazis	DNVP	DVP	CENTRE	DDP	SDP	USPD	KPD
Feb. 1919–June 1919	Scheidemann (SPD)				■	■	■		
June 1919–March 1920	Bauer (SPD)				■	■	■		
March 1920–June 1920	Müller (SPD)				■	■	■		
June 1920–May 1921	Fehrenbach (Centre)			■	■	■			
May 1921–Oct. 1921	Wirth (Centre)				■	■	■		
Oct. 1921–Nov. 1922	Wirth (Centre)				■	■	■		
Nov. 1922–Aug. 1923	Cuno (non-party)			■	■	■			
Aug. 1923–Oct. 1923	Stresemann (DVP)			■	■	■	■		
Oct. 1923–Nov. 1923	Stresemann (DVP)			■	■	■	■		
Nov. 1923–June 1924	Marx (Centre)			■	■	■			
June 1924–Jan. 1925	Marx (Centre)			■	■	■			
Jan. 1925–Dec. 1925	Luther (non-party)		■	■	■				
Dec. 1925–May 1926	Luther (non-party)			■	■	■			
May 1926–Dec. 1926	Marx (Centre)			■	■	■			
Jan. 1927–June 1928	Marx (Centre)		■	■	■				
June 1928–March 1930	Müller (SPD)			■	■	■	■		

NOTES
(i) Excluded from the table are Ebert's SPD–USPD 'Council of People's Commissars' (Nov. 1918–Feb. 1919) and the five 'Presidential' or 'Article 48' governments which were in office between 1930 and 1933: Brüning's first administration (March 1930–Oct. 1931), Brüning's second administration (Oct. 1931–May 1932), von Papen's administration (June 1932–Dec. 1932), Schleicher's administration (Dec. 1932–Jan. 1933), Hitler's administration (entered office Jan. 1933).
(ii) The names which the four different types of coalition which held office in the years 1919–33 were known by are:
　　the 'Weimar' coalition (Centre–DDP–SPD)
　　the 'middle-class' coalition (DVP–Centre–DDP)
　　the 'right-wing' coalition (DNVP–DVP–Centre)
　　the 'grand' coalition (DVP–Centre–DDP–SDP)

Table 4: Industrial production, 1918–33

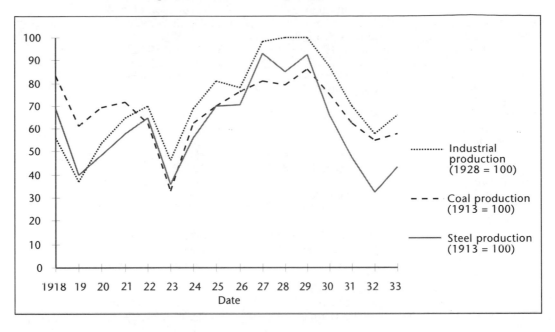

Table 5: Trade, 1925–33

	1925	1926	1927	1928	1929	1930	1931	1932	1933
Exports (by volume 1913 = 100)	66.4	76.7	77.4	87.4	98.0	92.2	82.7	55.6	50.7
Imports (by volume 1913 = 100)	82.3	72.5	105.2	101.7	96.6	86.0	69.9	62.5	62.8

Table 6: Unemployment, 1921–33

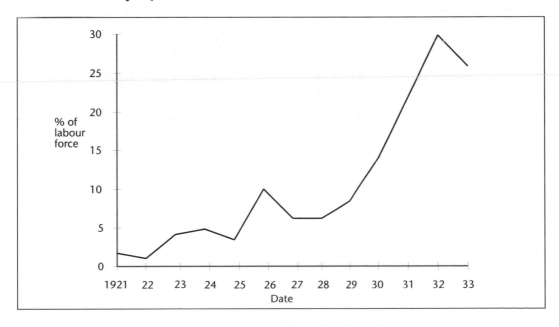